Seven Foundations of Time Mastery for Attorneys
by Julie A. Fleming, J.D.

Copyright © 2011 Julie A. Fleming, J.D.
All rights reserved. No part of this book may be reproduced in any means, print or electronic, without consent of:
Julie A. Fleming, J.D.
jaf@lifeatthebar.com
800.758.6214

Published by:
Crow Creek Press
Atlanta GA

Designed and typeset by:
Razor Edge Press
Bayville NJ

ISBN 978-0-9774018-8-8
Library of Congress Number: 2011935110
Printed in the United States of America by Lightning Source, LaVergne TN

Seven Foundations of Time Mastery for Attorneys

Julie A. Fleming, J.D.

Atlanta

 Seven Foundations of Time Mastery for Attorneys

Seven Foundations of Time Mastery for Attorneys

Table of Contents

Acknowledgements 11
Online Resources 13
Chapter One
   Introduction 15
Chapter Two
   The Genesis of *Seven Foundations* 19
Chapter Three
   Master Your Time 23
   Introducing the Seven Foundations of Time Mastery for Attorneys 24
   Getting Started with the Seven Foundations 26
Chapter Four
Foundation 1: Manage Your Energy, Not Your Time 29
   Manage Your Energy: Become a Legal Athlete 30
   Build Your Energy 31
   Reach Peak Performance 41
   Case Study 42
Chapter Five
Foundation 2: Set Priorities and Act Accordingly 45
   Step One: Create a Master To–Do List 46
   Step Two: Prioritize 49
      The Four Quadrant Method of Prioritization 50
   Step Three: Devise a Plan to Accomplish Your Tasks 57
   Step Four: Execute Your Plan Effectively 58
      Multi–Tasking: Don't Do It 58
      Use the Quadrants to Manage Interruptions 61

　　　Recover from Interruptions 62
　　　Block Your Time 63

Chapter Six
Foundation 3: Delegate Effectively 66
　　　The Top Five Mistakes in Delegating Work 67
　　　Avoid the Mistakes and Become an Excellent Delegator 70
　　　Identify Tasks to Delegate 74
　　　Get Extra Assistance 76

Chapter Seven
Foundation 4: Manage Your Physical Environment 78
　　　Office Environment 78
　　　Managing Paper 79
　　　Reducing Paper Clutter 79
　　　Filing Strategies for Paper 83

Chapter Eight
Foundation 5: Tame the Email Tsunami 86
　　　Handling the Email You Receive 88
　　　Sending Email 94
　　　　　Decide Whether to Send an Email 95
　　　　　Address Email and Name Recipients 97
　　　　　Use a Descriptive Subject Line 98
　　　　　Limit the Content of the Email 101
　　　Ask Questions Clearly 103
　　　Reply to Email 104
　　　Retaining Email Messages 105
　　　Dealing with Email Attachments 106
　　　Reaching In–Box Empty 106
　　　Working with PDAs 109
　　　Email Caveats 111
　　　Email and Personal Connections 112

Chapter Nine
Foundation 6: Work the Telephone 113
　　　Managing Telephone Calls 113
　　　Voicemail 115

Chapter Ten
Foundation 7: Set SMART Goals 118
Chapter Eleven
Conclusion 122
Additional Resources 129
Appendix 131

Dedicated to SHF and JDF

Acknowledgements

When I released the first edition of *Five Foundations of Time Mastery for Attorneys* in 2008, I had been consulting with attorneys for just over two years. Help with time management was a top client request, and I discovered that most clients could recognize significant benefits by making relatively small tweaks in their schedules.

Fast forward to 2011. Three years has created a massive change in the legal economy, and it seems safe to say that there is no hope of going back to the salad days. Lawyers (like everyone else) have become accustomed to doing more with less and squeezing maximum output from every moment. Even more, the downturn in the economy has produced a culture of rainmaking stronger than ever before. Time management has always been a key skill for lawyers, and economic pressures have brought an even brighter spotlight to this topic. I chose to update *Five Foundations* to offer suggestions relevant to today's circumstances and to include additional strategies developed over the last three years: enter *Seven Foundations of Time Mastery for Attorneys*.

I am grateful to the many clients who have shared their challenges and solutions with me and have allowed me into their practices to help them build better practices to better serve their clients. My bias cannot be overstated: the vast majority of attorneys seek to do well while doing good. It is my privilege to partner with my clients and to offer strategies and education to support their mission.

To those who have taught me so much about practice, business, and life, I offer deep gratitude: Sidney Howell Fleming, M.D., J. D. Fleming, Jr., the Honorable J. Owen Forrester, and R. Keegan Federal. This book (and its predecessor, *The Reluctant Rainmaker: A Guide for Lawyers Who Hate Selling*) would not exist without the careful attention and shepherding of Terri Wiebenga and Vicky Likens. I couldn't dream up more highly skilled and fun partners. Thank you for all of your efforts! Finally, I appreciate the support, encouragement, and feedback of dear friends and colleagues: Jory Fisher, Nikki Incandela, Bryn Johnson, Monica Parker, Robin Samora, Margo Shoemaker, and many more.

Brilliance herein is reflected from my many teachers; mistakes are mine entirely.

Julie A. Fleming
Atlanta, Georgia
May 2011

Seven Foundations of Time Mastery for Attorneys

Online Resources

Please visit **www.SevenFoundations.com** to access additional resources for use with *Seven Foundations of Time Mastery for Attorneys*. The resources include audio recordings and transcripts for the Time Mastery Inner Circle, a 2008—2009 coaching group.

Inner Circle topics include:

- How to Network without Leaving the Office
- How to Have a Thriving Practice that Leaves Time for Summer Fun
- How to Create a Newsletter without Running Yourself Ragged
- How to Accomplish More in Less Time by Working with Virtual Assistants
- Speaking and Writing to Get Results: How to Speak and Write to Get Clients or a New Job So That You Can do the Work Once and Watch the Benefit Accrue
- Social Media: An Interview with the LinkedIn Lawyer
- Remember Me? How to Follow Up with Contacts Effectively, Efficiently, and Inexpensively
- Master Your Time to Master Your Goals

- Procrastination: Use It Effectively or Eliminate It!
- How to Find and Deliver Information to Wow (and Woo) Your Clients… in Less Than Ten Minutes a Day

You will also find a Resource Rolodex of products and services that my clients and I have used to assist in saving time, effort, money, or a combination of the three. These "go to" resources will provide support as you seek to become more efficient and effective in how you use your time.

Chapter One

Introduction

How often do you feel overwhelmed by all you need to do and all you need to *remember* to do? Most of us have long lists of tasks that we have to accomplish, often supplemented by the mental list that we maintain but never write down. Much of the time, our tracking system is sufficient to keep things moving forward and to catch the tasks that nearly slip through the cracks. But sometimes things do slide, and we end up embarrassed, overworked, or stressed out (maybe all three) as we try to fix the resulting problems.

Underneath the task of remembering all the tasks lies the substantive work itself. There's talking with clients, writing memoranda and other documents, reviewing and editing the same, talking with colleagues and opposing counsel, setting schedules, researching, analyzing, planning and preparing—just to name a few of the tasks that most lawyers do every single day. Add in administrative work (completing timesheets, billing, expense reports, paying invoices), professional development (reading advance sheets, attending CLE programs, reviewing publications relevant to your clients and practice), client development (entertaining clients, writing articles and blog posts, speaking, drafting newsletter and website copy, revising your biographical sketch, networking, following up with new contacts, asking for business, preparing pitch documents, and more)... Is it any wonder that so many attorneys are worn out, stressed out, or even burned out?

Seven Foundations of Time Mastery for Attorneys

And then there's 20th century kudzu[1]: email. Email was initially a quick, convenient way to communicate. After its explosion in popularity and the initiation of spam, email has become an irritation that can consume hours or even days. Email threads its way through every aspect of practice and, thanks to smartphones, can invade every waking moment if permitted. Email seems to be the omnipresent convenience that both facilitates simple communications and requires extra hours to handle those simple communications.

> **The lawyer who is able to separate the "must do" from the "could do" and the "must know" from the "nice to know" will be in a better position to build a successful practice that serves clients well, contributes to the legal community, and yields a satisfying and sustainable career.**

Identified as a "jealous mistress" by Joseph Story long before the advent of the 2000-billable-hour requirement that is now common (and, for many firms, an understatement of actual expectations), the practice of law demands numerous hours and seemingly endless attention. Technology, heralded as the answer, often has simply made it possible to do more work in the same amount of time—and in some cases, technology has even increased the amount of work to be handled. (Remember when we believed, perhaps foolishly, that email would make work quicker and easier? Do you dare to imagine how many hours

---

[1] Kudzu is a Japanese plant that was introduced to the United States in 1876. Gardeners seized on the beautiful, large-leafed vine with the sweet blossoms and imported it into the Southeastern U.S., where it was hailed as good food for animals and an attractive way to prevent soil erosion. However, kudzu has been too successful, growing as much as a foot a day in the summer months and choking out other vegetation.

you spent managing email just in the last week?) Technology has relieved some symptoms of overwhelm and overwork but frequently exacerbates the underlying problem of too many activities and too little time.

Today's economy and market present new opportunities, however, and a new model for success. We are no longer discussing how to do the same things more efficiently or how to cram more activity into a day. Instead, today's successful attorney is the one who sets priorities most effectively and executes her plans accordingly. In a world in which no one can expect to have it all or do it all, the lawyer who is able to separate the "must do" from the "could do" and the "must know" from the "nice to know" will be in a better position to build a successful practice that serves clients well, contributes to the legal community, and yields a satisfying and sustainable career.

In this new world, technology becomes the servant, not the master. Technology and old-school organizational tactics can be combined to keep track of that endless list of tasks, and relatively small shifts in habit can generate refreshed energy. These tactics and shifts are the basis of *Seven Foundations of Time Mastery for Attorneys*. As you discover how to revive time-tested tactics and bring them into today's technological context, you will discover how to use your time as effectively as possible.

> You must use your time rather than allowing your hours and days to consume you.

When you master how you use time, you will be able to identify and (on most days) achieve your top priority. You will close your days, most days, with the knowledge that you accomplished what needed to be done, you processed the communications and information that came your way, and you will do so in a way that honors your values and the life you want to lead. Sure, you will have the occasional day when chaos hits, but even on those days, you will know what to do to manage the chaos and to restore order. You will use your

time rather than allowing your hours and days to consume you.

Seven Foundations of Time Mastery for Attorneys introduces seven basic principles that, used in concert, will allow you to change the way you think about time. The foundations are simple:

- Manage your energy, not your time
- Set priorities and act accordingly
- Delegate effectively
- Manage your physical environment
- Tame the email tsunami
- Work the telephone
- Set SMART goals

When you implement these Seven Foundations and the practices subsumed within each of them, you will reshape the way you think about and use time. You will reduce your stress level, you will increase your productivity, and you will make time for the things that matter most to you in your practice and in your life. Hundreds of lawyers have experienced these results, and now you can too.

A word about client stories included:

Because client confidentiality is paramount in all coaching and consulting engagements, the stories included herein represent composite clients, with names and other identifying details changed.

Chapter Two

The Genesis of *Seven Foundations*

Advice and teaching is only as good as its source, so before I share the time mastery and organizational suggestions that I developed over my nearly 20 years in practice, I will share my background and how I developed the strategies and skills shared in *Seven Foundations*.

I graduated from the Emory School of Law in 1993 and served a two-year federal clerkship. Through that work, I decided that I wanted to practice patent litigation. Because I had an English degree and no technical background, I returned to college to get a Bachelor's degree in biology to meet the prerequisites to sit for the patent bar. During that time, I practiced part-time, doing contract work for general litigation and intellectual property law firms. After becoming a registered patent attorney, I practiced patent litigation with a sole practitioner for about a year and then moved to the Atlanta office of Jones Day, where I was in practice for nearly six years. I then moved to a mid-sized intellectual property firm in Orlando, Florida, before founding Life at the Bar LLC in 2005. I am also Of Counsel with Federal & Hasson LLP, an Atlanta litigation boutique, though my practice is now quite limited.

I excelled in juggling responsibilities while in college and law school, and as you might imagine, serving a clerkship was a fairly low-stress way to

 *Seven Foundations of Time Mastery for Attorneys*

begin practice in terms of time management. Although chambers had some crunch times, the work usually lacked the pressure of practice. Complications started to appear while I was practicing part-time and managing a full-time schedule of "round two" college classes, including lectures and laboratories. At times I felt as if I had to cram 36 hours of work into each 24-hour day. I was relieved when I began working full-time with a sole practitioner; even though we had several trials, at least I was able to focus on one kind of task at a time. And then I moved to Jones Day.

Some readers may have heard that the nickname for Jones Day is "Jones Days, Nights, and Weekends." I didn't find that to be generally accurate, but the volume of work and the level of responsibility were formidable. I learned then that prioritization is the foundation of accomplishment. In a sort of trial by fire, I learned what interruptions merited my attention, how to delegate, and how to manage the various assignments I had going on at any given time so that I was able to get done what I needed to get done when I needed to get it done. I also learned that using time effectively often requires letting unimportant things go undone.

My primary goal, of course, was to do exceptional work for my clients (internal and external) and to advance my technical legal skill. My secondary goal was to reduce the number of nights and weekends that I was working unnecessarily. I never wanted to be working at midnight, of course, and I quickly discovered that late nights and weekends in the office were unbearably painful when they resulted from my own lack of time management. Looking back, business development should have been a focus even in those early years, but as I discuss in *The Reluctant Rainmaker: A Guide for Lawyers Who Hate Selling*, that activity came into play only after my fifth year of practice.

I started to develop my own brand of time mastery—sometimes informed by CLE programs and practice management articles, and always refined by trial and error. Working at Jones Day gave me access to a stellar support staff, which taught me not only how to manage my own time, but also how to delegate and leverage my time through their efforts. When I moved to a smaller firm in Orlando, I had to revise my habits because the support staff—still a talented group—left the office by 5:30 every day, and I couldn't count on leaving a project to be finished overnight by someone else while I slept. I had to adapt what I knew about prioritization and delegation in order to make the most of the help that was available.

When I opened Life at the Bar in 2005, colleagues congratulated me on choosing to pursue great work/life balance. Fortunately, that goal had not been any part of my reason for launching my own business, and I quickly learned that wearing every hat (service provider, CEO, COO, IT staff, receptionist, administrative assistant, and more) meant that time would be at more of a premium than ever before. I had to revise my habits to get everything done through my own efforts, initially with no support staff.

I spent the first two years developing systems and learning to automate as much as possible. When I finally hired a virtual assistant in 2007, I had to change my operating approach, this time without any blueprint for which tasks should be delegated and which reserved for my effort alone. Since then, my team has expanded and I now have an operations manager who directs a staff of three to five assistants. Others handle the administrative pieces of my business, leaving me free to do the work only I can do: consulting and coaching, training, speaking, writing, and marketing by making personal contacts. I now do very little non–billable work other than business development activities, leaving me time to plan strategically for the growth of my business. My work flows more smoothly, and the increased billable work I can do more than covers my assistants' monthly fees.

I use the Seven Foundations every single day. Like most people, I stumble at times and need to readjust and adapt my habits to changing circumstances. However, a few circumstances are consistent. I no longer worry that I will miss deadlines or jolt myself awake with fear if a task is left undone. If I am working at midnight, I do so only because the wee hours are a particularly creative time for me, not because I am putting in extraordinary hours to cope with overwhelming tasks. Is it perfect? No. I am human. But I know that the Seven Foundations framework works for me, and I know that

I will be able to work through whatever challenges crop up by applying the strategies and tactics that have been so successful to this point.

The beauty of the Seven Foundations lies in their simplicity and their flexibility. (And, incidentally, that is why this is the *Seven* Foundations—who wants to wade through a 300–page treatise on using time? Better to focus on a small number of principles that will have significant impact.) Ready to learn more? Great! Let's get started.

Chapter Three

Master Your Time

Although most people use the phrase "time management," no one can actually *manage* time. The phrase "time management" suggests that if only we do the right things and we do them in the right order, or we add some trick that we are not using now, at last, magically, we will be able to manage time. Finally, we will have more time.

Of course, that just is not so. We cannot create time. Whether time is used productively or frittered away, we all have 24 hours in each day. It would be terrific if we could find a way to create more hours in a day—indeed, the ability to do so would finally lay to rest all of the lawyer jokes that revolve around unscrupulous attorneys who bill 35 hours in each day! Alas, it is just not possible.

The phrase I prefer instead is *time mastery*. Mastering time means accomplishing the right things at the right time. Through time mastery and by using the techniques presented in *Seven Foundations of Time Mastery for Attorneys*, you will get more done in the same number of hours, and more importantly, you will ensure that you are getting the right things done in the proper order. You will serve your clients more effectively and more efficiently. Client satisfaction with your work will go up, as will your own satisfaction. You may see an increase in referrals as a result. If your practice is amenable to repeat business, you will likely see an increase because clients appreciate lawyers who use their time well. Last but certainly not least, you will likely have more success in rainmaking simply because you will create more opportunities to do the activities that lead to bringing in new cases and clients. You will not shortchange your client development time in an effort to get your billable work done. Instead, having prioritized your activities, delegated effectively, and leveraged your time well, you will be able to dedicate time to the activities that lead to business.

All of these benefits, and more, flow from time mastery. Master your time so you are doing the things that need to be done when they need to be done and doing them effectively. When you master your time, you increase the opportunities for making more money. You have happier clients. You feel less stress. You build a sustainable practice. And you enjoy that practice more.

Introducing the Seven Foundations of Time Mastery for Attorneys

Time mastery breaks down into seven foundational principles, on which numerous techniques and strategies rest. Energy management lies at the center of time mastery. As energy is created, expended, and renewed, other skills come into play. Prioritization is fundamental to ensuring that the right things are done at the right time. Effective delegation facilitates work flow, as does appropriate organization of the physical environment and careful communications. Finally, goal setting serves as a compass to keep your work on course.

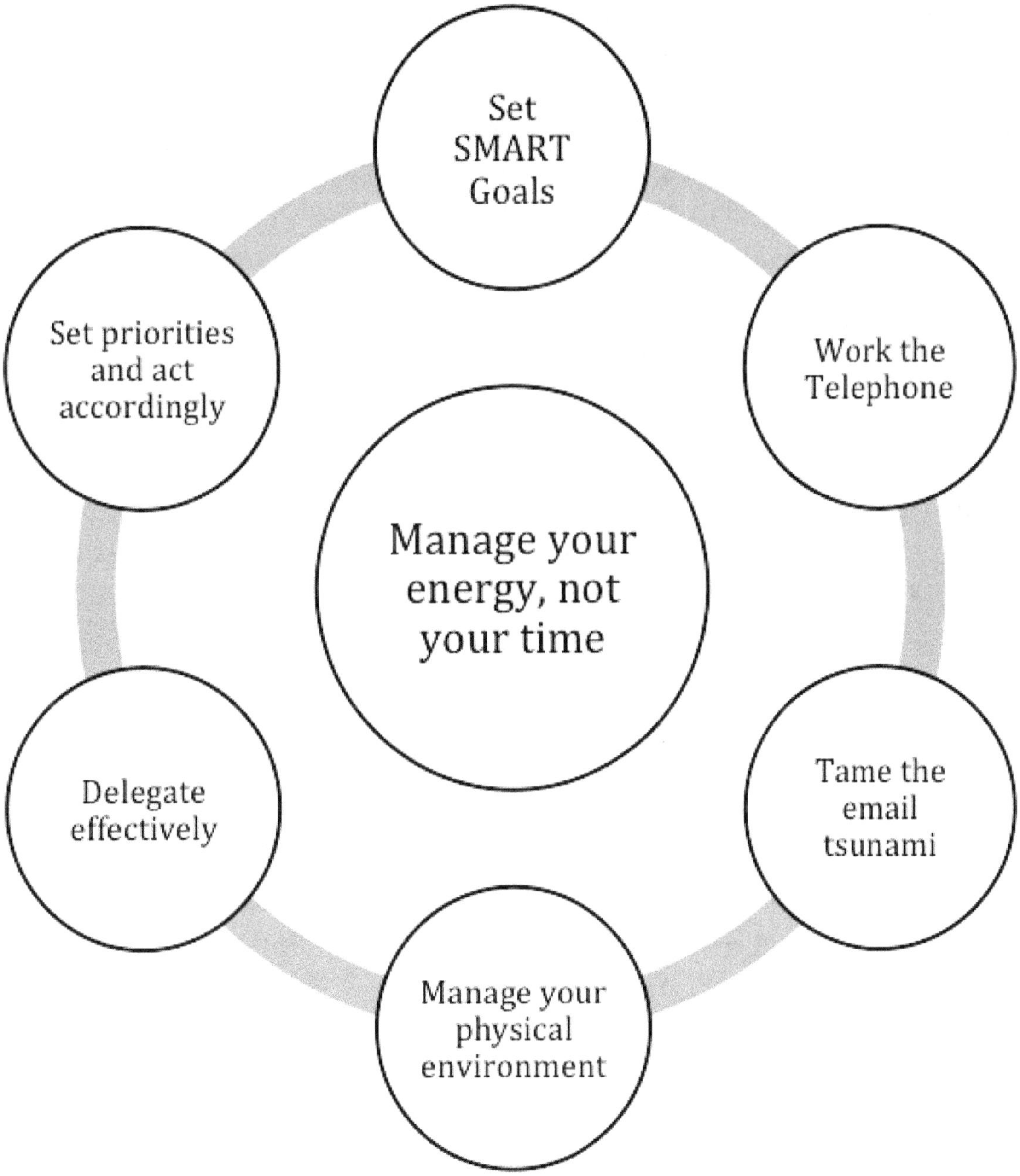

Seven Foundations of Time Mastery for Attorneys

- Set SMART Goals
- Work the Telephone
- Tame the email tsunami
- Manage your physical environment
- Delegate effectively
- Set priorities and act accordingly

Manage your energy, not your time

Getting Started with the Seven Foundations

To get the maximum benefit from this system, I encourage you to read through each section and flag the steps that you can apply to your practice immediately. Notice the suggestions that prompt you to think, "I could never do that!" While some of the ideas presented here will not work for your practice or your preferences, an idea that brings on a strong reaction often serves as a signal to do a little digging to discover why your reaction is so strong. You might find useful information in the reaction, or you might discover ways in which your contrary habits are not serving you.

Interspersed in these materials you will find exercises that allow you to personalize the techniques to match your own practice and your needs. Be sure you complete those exercises. Just as watching a golf game on TV will not improve your swing, merely reading this material will not be effective to help you master your time. You must engage with the material, choose which changes you want to make, and take the steps necessary to break old habits and to adopt new ones.

Every attorney, without exception, can implement the Seven Foundations into his practice. However, not every attorney will do so, and those who do so only half-heartedly will reap only partial rewards. Lawyers who fail to incorporate the Seven Foundations into their daily habits will fall short for one or more of the following reasons.

1. **Negative beliefs:** *"Maybe this stuff will not work for me."* Hundreds of lawyers have used the Seven Foundations. Because every practice, every personality, and every set of preferences is unique, not all of the tactics or approaches suggested will work for every person. However, if you experiment with the Foundations and test to see which, perhaps unexpectedly, work best for you, you will most likely discover at least a handful that change the way you think about, schedule, and use your time. Not all of "this stuff" has to work for you to experience a significant shift.

2. **Lack of a role model:** *"No one I work with runs their practice this way!"*

Seven Foundations of Time Mastery for Attorneys

We all know that any change is easier with a role model or a mentor. However, the reason you purchased this book is, presumably, because something in your practice is not functioning as well as you would like it to function. Why sabotage the potential for turning things around simply because no one else is using the same approach? *Seven Foundations of Time Mastery for Attorneys* is designed to function as your guide and even your mentor. With step–by–step directions and worksheets that allow you to customize each suggestion for your practice, this book will serve as your guide for effective use of time.

3. **Intransigence**: *"I tried the Foundations for a few days and nothing changed."* Change is challenging. Studies show that few patients follow medical advice to make taxing changes (losing weight, stopping the use of tobacco, and increasing activity, for example) even when faced with the prospect of death. Imagine, then, how heavy the burden of inertia may be when the changes at hand are less urgent. Keep consistent change as the theme of your Seven Foundations experiment. Try something new for a week or two weeks, reward yourself for consistent implementation, and then decide whether you want to maintain that effort going forward. Some experiments you will keep, others you will modify or discard, and with consistent effort over time you will see real changes in your practice and yourself.

4. **Lack of commitment**: You may find that even experiments are "too demanding." Why do you want to change the way you use your time? If you only want to improve an already–functional approach to time, more effort will probably be required to take on an experiment. If you picked up *Seven Foundations* because your time is out of control, or if you are missing deadlines and dropping client responsibilities, your motivation is likely to be substantially greater.

 What is your "big why" for wanting to improve the way you use your time? Is there a *bigger* "big why" that draws you? Use this space to note your fundamental reasons for wanting to improve your time management (or mastery), and refer back if you notice your resolve slipping.

_____
_____
_____
_____
_____
_____
_____

5. **Lack of time**: You must spend time reading *Seven Foundations* and implementing the suggestions. You will learn nothing by osmosis, and placing this book on your desk will not change a thing for you. Block out time right now (three hours should be more than sufficient) to read this book and work through the exercises. Write down your committed "study time" and time for implementation here and on your calendar:

_____

Although these obstacles are real, each can be overcome. More specifically, *you* can overcome any of these obstacles that threaten to keep you trapped in habits that are not working. You will stumble from time to time as you work to change the way you think about and use your time, but within these pages you will find everything you need to make the shift you are seeking.

Chapter Four

Foundation 1: Manage Your Energy, Not Your Time

The First Foundation of Time Mastery for Attorneys focuses on managing energy, not time. The reason is simple: no matter how much time you have, without sufficient energy to perform at a high level during that time, you will not be able to accomplish much.

Think about a day when you came into the office with very low energy. Maybe you had a bad headache, or perhaps you were facing a difficult personal situation. Or possibly you were up too late the night before or just had a bad night of sleep. Whatever the cause, your efficiency and effectiveness were probably both below par, dragging right along with your energy. If you had a big deadline, you probably summoned the strength to meet it (because that is what professionals do), but your routine work most likely suffered somewhat, especially if you tried to do anything that called for complex thought or deep concentration. Even if you decided to stay in the office later than usual, you probably did not accomplish as much as you would have liked, and chances are good that the quality of your work was not up to your usual standards.

Energy management is the foundational currency of work. Without energy, time is almost meaningless.

Manage Your Energy: Become a Legal Athlete

In the Harvard Business Review article, "The Making of a Corporate Athlete,"[1] Jim Loehr and Tony Schwartz compare an athlete with a businessperson. The authors argued that athletes' work is based on a cycle that oscillates between the training season, the game season, and the off-season. During the training season, the athlete is building up and preparing for the game season. During the game season, the athlete plays hard and plays to win. When an athlete is "on," she is *completely* on: at the peak of physical, mental, and emotional ability, all focused on achieving and winning the game at hand. Following the game season and the focused expenditure of so much energy, the athlete moves to an off-season for rest, recovery, and a recharge of energy. And then the cycle begins again. (Note that this cycle occurs daily as well as over a period of weeks or months.)

In contrast, Loehr and Schwartz argue, those who work in business hold themselves to a "higher" standard. Each day brings a new game season in business, frequently without adequate "off-season" rest. Particularly with the expectation of nearly round-the-clock availability and the technological tethers that interrupt personal time as much as they facilitate time away from the office, lawyers face a string of workdays with little time for renewal between them. The risk is that, unlike the athlete who had plenty of time to rest, re-energize, and train for game day, lawyers lack the full energy that fuels peak performance. With some exceptions for critical events like a negotiation or the deadline for drafting a critical document, "game day" for lawyers is just another hard day's work, probably sandwiched between two more of the same.

Imagine that you keep a pitcher of water on your desk and refill it every morning so you can drink from it during the day. Imagine that on a Tuesday, you only drank about half of the water in the pitcher, and that

---

[1] Jim Loehr, Tony Schwartz Harvard Business Review (January 2001). A link to the article is available at www.SevenFoundations.com.

when you come in on Wednesday you decide not to refill it. Through Wednesday morning, you might drink water at the usual pace. At some point during the day, you will run out of water. No matter how intensely you might try to coax more water from the pitcher, the best you could get would be a drop or two. You would not get enough water to quench your thirst without refilling the pitcher. Out of water is out of water, however much you might wish or pretend otherwise.

Likewise, out of energy is out of energy. Except under special circumstances when you experience a physiological reaction to something that provokes the "fight or flight" response and unleashes a jolt of adrenaline on your system, you cannot coax energy from yourself if you have not "refilled the pitcher." (And, by the way, even if you do get the jolt of adrenaline, it lasts a short time and generally causes even lower energy when its effects wear off.)

Managing energy requires oscillation between working at peak performance (a state that Loehr and Schwartz call "full engagement") and taking time to recharge energy through rest and meaningful recreation ("selective disengagement"). Like athletes, lawyers must learn how to sustain and effectively use energy during work, and how to rest, refresh, and re-energize during specifically planned non-work times.

Build Your Energy

Loehr and Schwartz identify four sources of energy that must be present for optimum, sustainable performance: physical, emotional, mental, and purposeful.[2] Practicing law demands energy in each of these domains, which build on one another as shown in the following diagram.

---

[2] Jim Loehr and Tony Schwartz, *The Power of Full Engagement* (Free Press 2003) at 9–10. The authors use the phrase "spiritual energy" rather than purposeful energy.

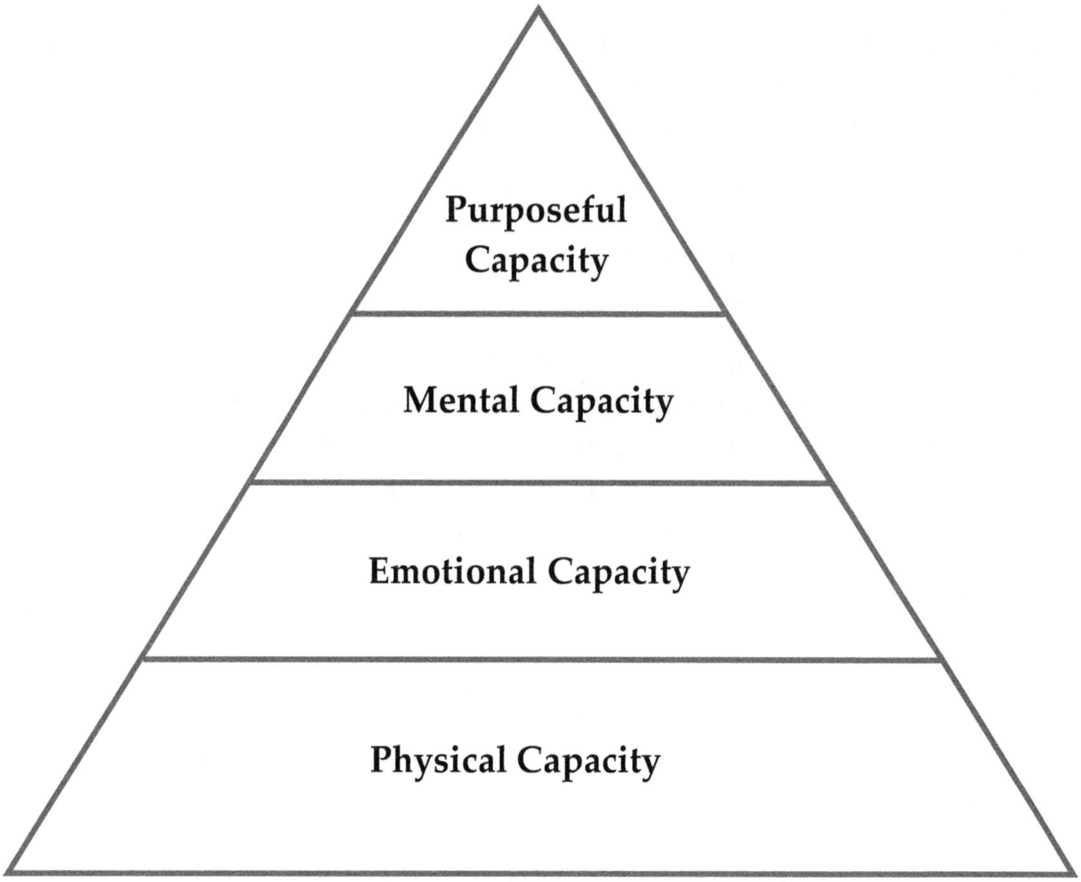

```
         Purposeful
          Capacity

        Mental Capacity

       Emotional Capacity

        Physical Capacity
```

Physical capacity can be fueled or drained. I often refer to the physical fuels as the "family rules," because most of us had mothers or fathers who insisted we do the things that fuel physical energy. Physical fuels include getting enough sleep, exercising regularly, drinking water, eating nutritiously, and breathing properly. None of these are surprising, but lawyers under stress tend to discard these habits too quickly, preferring (for example) to skimp on sleep and get in a few more hours of work instead, or to drink coffee all day instead of water. Physical drains tend to be the crutches we use when we are not feeling energetic, like caffeine or sugar we might use to get a quick lift. Some of the drains do deliver that lift, but all of them ultimately lead to a crash in energy.

 The table below lists some common physical fuels and drains. Personalize the list by adding your own fuels and drains. For example, maybe you have noticed that playing a particular song can recharge your energy. Put it on the list.

Physical Energy Fuels	Physical Energy Drains
Sufficient sleep	Sugar
Regular exercise	Caffeine
Drinking water	Relying on adrenaline
Nutritious foods	Time wasters (mindless TV, aimless web surfing)
Breathing deeply	

Physical capacity also increases through oscillation between expenditure of energy and recovery. In other words, your professional performance and your effectiveness at work will improve if you commit to selectively disengaging from your work at predefined times by removing yourself physically, mentally, and emotionally from the office. Create time in which you are not working and not thinking about work. Instead, identify activities that you enjoy and that leave you feeling refreshed.

A vacation is an extended example of selective disengagement—*if* you truly disengage from your work, though not if you remain tied to the telephone and checking email and doing "just a little work" that grows to occupy your time. However, an annual or biannual vacation is insufficient to create the oscillation between engagement and disengagement that maximizes energy. Instead, you must find ways to incorporate downtime into each day. Make an appointment with yourself to work out, to visit a museum, to read, to spend some time in nature, or to do whatever works best for you.

Simply making an appointment is often not enough, though. You must claim and protect the time you create for yourself. Do not wait for someone at your law firm, government office, or corporation to say, "Hey, you've worked really hard. Go home." Clients' experience has proved that in the unlikely event you receive that message, you will get a follow-up immediately afterward asking you to return to the office. If you do not *take* your personal time, nobody else will prompt you to do so.

Sole practitioners may be wondering how to keep a practice going while spending selective disengagement time away from the office. Clear communication with your clients and opposing counsel (where relevant) will go a long way to freeing time for yourself, as long as you enforce the boundaries you set. For example, you might decide that you are not available after 7 P.M., absent a true emergency. If you accept a telephone call from a client (or, worse yet, place a call to a client) after 7 P.M. to address a non-emergency issue, you will demonstrate that you do not *really* mean that you are unavailable, and you can expect post-7 P.M. communications to become more and more frequent. Instead, block out your personal time and protect those appointments as sacred.

A second tactic that will help in generating free time is delegating work to a trusted assistant. Chapter Six addresses not only what and how to delegate, but also how to get help without hiring an employee.

Seven Foundations of Time Mastery for Attorneys

 **Define what you would like your ordinary working hours to be, leaving some time for a midday break for lunch, working out, or another activity that refuels you. (Note that a midday break can be as short as ten or fifteen minutes. A "lunch hour" is often a good investment of time toward a productive afternoon, but if an hour seems unreasonable, start with a smaller block of time and experiment to see what results come to pass.)**

_____
_____
_____
_____
_____

When did you last take a vacation? If it has been a while (or if you feel the need even if you were on a vacation recently), commit to taking at least a long weekend within the next two months. Consult with your spouse or partner, check your schedule, and block out a time for relaxation. Write the dates and where you plan to go (or what you plan to do if you would prefer a "staycation").

_____
_____
_____
_____
_____

Emotional capacity refers to the extent that you are able to experience positive emotions and to avoid coming into the office in a bad mood or in a funk because of a lack of energy. Emotional and physical energy are dependent on one another: a lack of physical energy often leads to negative emotions, and both positive and negative emotions have physical impact due to the associated release of hormones. Negative emotions such as fear, anger, and frustration tend to promote the release of stress hormones that cause physical symptoms of stress. Limiting negative emotions is associated with emotional capacity, and strong emotional capacity is associated with reduced stress. Competencies such as self-control, self-confidence, good interpersonal communications, and empathy tend to promote emotional capacity.

Because stress cannot be completely eliminated and challenging circumstances may produce negative emotions, "recovery activities" are important to maintaining strong emotional capacity. Recovery activities might include meditation, singing, doing yoga, dancing, writing, playing soccer, or spending time with friends and family. The key is to ensure that whatever activity you do is deeply pleasurable, enjoyable, and fulfilling to you. You must also ensure that you engage in the activity regularly.

One exercise that encourages emotional renewal is a simple "centering" practice. Sit comfortably upright in a chair, with legs uncrossed and your feet on the ground, hands resting lightly on your thighs. Close your eyes, inhale slowly, hold your breath for a beat, and then exhale slowly. Allow your mind to clear as you breathe, perhaps focusing on the words "in" and "out" to match your breath. When thoughts arise, and they will, simply notice and release them. Take two to five minutes (or more) to allow your body, your thoughts, and your emotions to calm. If you practice regularly, preferably once or twice a day, you will also find that simply taking a few deep breaths will bring you to a calm state even when you are under stress.

Seven Foundations of Time Mastery for Attorneys

 What activities renew your emotional capacity? List several here, and consider when and how often you would like to engage in the activities. For maximum impact, schedule a few recovery activities into your calendar now.

_____
_____
_____
_____
_____
_____
_____
_____

Mental capacity refers to the extent that you are able to focus on your work and to be truly engaged with your work. It means being fully present with your work (in other words, paying full attention to the task in front of you, not contemplating other "to do" items) and maintaining sustained high levels of concentration, as well as holding a realistically optimistic outlook about the outcome of your work. In addition, mental capacity generates the flexibility required to identify and examine a variety of points of view, and it permits you to switch between analytical and creative approaches to a challenge. Physical and mental energy are closely related: without sufficient physical energy, you will find it difficult to develop adequate mental energy over the long run.

Mental capacity and the optimism that characterizes it are critical, especially for lawyers. Much of a legal practice is problem–focused, such as looking critically at documents to find and eliminate problems before they

arise or working through litigation to resolve conflicts that have already arisen. As a result, lawyers tend to be both self-selected and trained to be pessimists. While pessimism may serve a client's needs in anticipating and avoiding trouble, a pessimistic approach to life can undermine an attorney's effectiveness as well as her enjoyment.

Expending and renewing mental energy increases mental capacity. Research shows that the limit on focused concentration is 60 to 90 minutes for most people. When my client Sara complained that she was ineffective during afternoons at work, I asked about her work patterns and learned that she had blocked out four hours each afternoon to focus on a large project. Halfway through that period, though, she would get tired and easily distracted, and her work product suffered. By dividing the four hours into three 75-minute blocks with ten minutes in between for walking around, stretching, and listening to music that made her feel good, Sara became more effective even though she was actually devoting slightly less time to her work. The difference? Increased mental energy, supported by infusions of physical fuel. (Worried about the reduction in the billable hours? By protecting her energy, Sara was able to bill more of her overall time at the office.)

Other methods to increase mental energy include the previously-described centering practice and meditation, both of which increase the concentration and focus that characterize mental capacity. Mental energy may also be enhanced by creative work, such as painting or dance. Creativity improves mental flexibility because it encourages you to get in touch with the analytical and intuitive approaches to work.

Visualization is a particularly good tool for in-the-moment renewal of energy. In fact, neurobiological research shows that visualization of an event prompts physiological changes in accord with the visualization. A basketball player who visualizes making a slam dunk will experience physical changes that would accompany that act, even though he will not actually jump up and dunk the ball. To bring this into a practice setting, think about an upcoming important meeting. How will the meeting go? What is the ideal outcome? What do you anticipate your adversary will say, and how will you respond? What points do you want to make ? Go into detail, and "see" the meeting in your mind. What are you wearing? How are you standing or sitting? What feelings are you experiencing? What do you hear?

Visualizing increases your mental engagement with the task at hand and will likely improve your performance, because visualizing is mentally practicing what you need to do to get your desired outcome. Mental rehearsals through visualization allow you to experience the fruits of your desired outcome both mentally and emotionally. Having prepped yourself for success in this manner, you are more likely to act in accord with what you have visualized. (Be careful: imagining disaster may create disaster. If you visualize tripping as you cross the floor to shake hands with an important new client for the first time, you may increase the chance of doing so when you actually meet.)

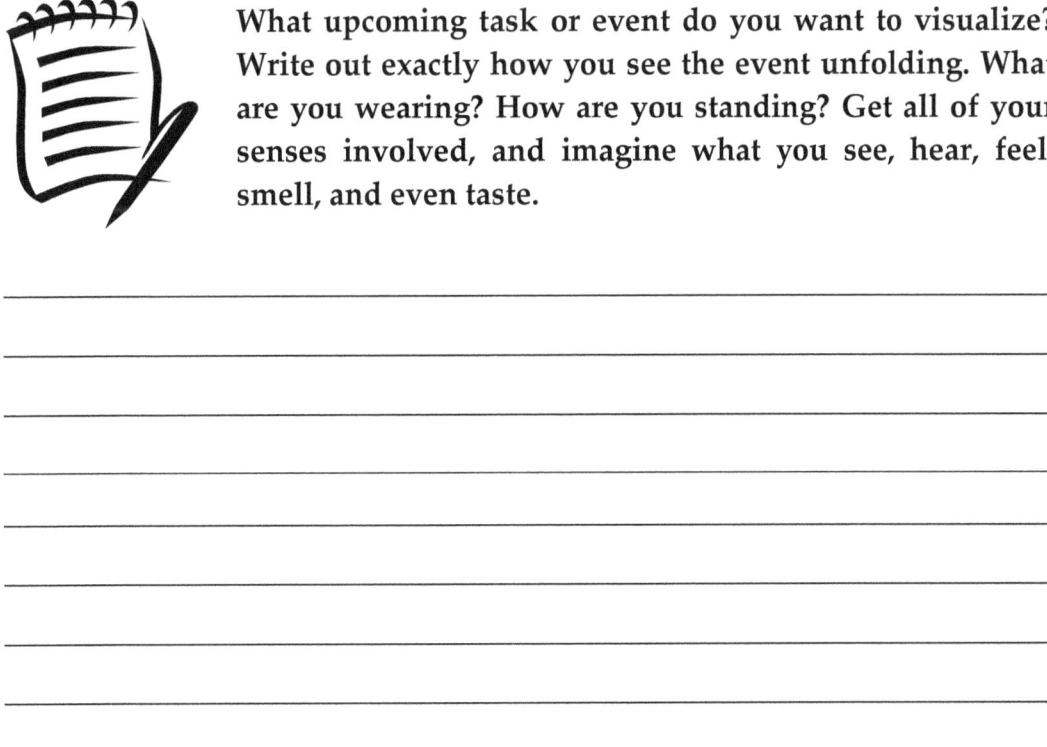

What upcoming task or event do you want to visualize? Write out exactly how you see the event unfolding. What are you wearing? How are you standing? Get all of your senses involved, and imagine what you see, hear, feel, smell, and even taste.

_____
_____
_____
_____
_____
_____
_____
_____

Purposeful capacity refers to the ability to bring your deepest values into your day–to–day life and to connect with the purpose for your work. Why did you go to law school? Why are you doing the work that you're doing? What matters most to you? What is your most important priority today, this week, or this year? What are your top values?

Knowing your values is important, but maximizing your purposeful capacity (and thus your energy) requires that you actually incorporate those values into your life. How can you express those values in the way you live and work? You may benefit from writing your top values or priorities onto a small card or sticky note, and then placing those notes near your computer, telephone, or calendar—anywhere that you are likely to look when making a decision about how to use time. Acting in accord with your values and priorities increases purposeful energy; acting in dissonance with them will decrease that energy.

You can increase purposeful energy through activity that inspires you, such as spending time in nature, reading a meaningful book, or listening to music. Spiritual practices such as prayer and meditation, as well as meditative exercise like yoga or tai chi, also work to increase purposeful energy. However, the best way to increase your purposeful energy is to engage in meaningful activity that connects you with your values.

Take a moment to write your top values and priorities. What is most important to you? (If you have never explored what your values are, consider purchasing and working through *Stand Up For Your Life* by Cheryl Richardson, which features a values exercise on pages 64–72.)

_____
_____
_____
_____

Seven Foundations of Time Mastery for Attorneys

 **Do you feel that you have an opportunity to express your values and priorities at work? If not, list three to five things you could do to connect with your values and priorities either through your work or through personal or *pro bono* pursuits.**

_____
_____
_____
_____
_____

Reach Peak Performance

When you put together physical capacity, emotional capacity, mental capacity, and purposeful capacity, you create the energy necessary to fuel peak performance. You will be able to get more done, no matter what strategies you are using, and to get the right things done at the right time. You will experience effective productivity. Focusing on energy management is critical because without this foundational piece, the techniques presented through the other six foundations of time mastery will lose effectiveness.

 **Now that you have identified how you can fuel yourself physically, emotionally, mentally, and purposefully, commit to doing so. List here the top five changes you would like to incorporate based on what you have learned so far. Then, turn to your calendar and schedule time for the activities you want to implement. Hold these appointments sacred: if you do not honor time for yourself, no one will.**

Case Study

Barbara hired me to work on time management and work/life balance, but we both quickly realized that the real work would address her energy management. I knew I had a challenge coming when I received an email from Barbara: "It's 4:27 AM and I'm sitting in my bathroom, checking email here so I won't disturb my husband's sleep. I've been here since 3:30, when I woke up in a panic. I am exhausted and I am overwhelmed. I need help with managing my time."

My coaching engagements begin with a consultation: the potential client and I will talk for about a half hour, long enough to give us each a good feel for the other person, to allow us both to determine whether I am the right person to help with the situation, and to let us decide whether the potential client is ready to take action and make necessary changes. During our initial consultation, Barbara, a successful lawyer who had been in practice for about 20 years, described her days in a weary voice. On the go all day and well into the evening, Barbara would typically leave home by 6:00 in the morning and most days she would not get home until 9:00 at night. She was tired, overwhelmed, and angry. She dreaded her days. Her relationships were suffering. She reported that her husband told her one day, "Even when you're home, on those rare occasions when you're not working, it's as if there's just a shell there and the rest of you is somewhere else—and I don't know where."

When I asked Barbara how she felt, she told me that she felt unfocused and disorganized. Moreover, she said, the support staff and the lawyers working with her also felt unfocused, disorganized, and frustrated with her constant activity because no one could get her full attention. She told me, "I love what I do. I'm good at it, my clients like me, and I like my clients, but I can't live like this. I can't keep doing what I'm doing. Something has to change or I'm going to burn out. Who am I kidding? I'm already burned out—I'm going to burn out all the way."

We worked together on energy management and addressed the four capacities. Barbara began protecting her physical capacity by deciding that she would take early morning or evening meetings only three days a week, and that she would not schedule those days back-to-back. She decided that she would ordinarily work between 8:30 A.M. and 7 P.M., that she would take 20 or 30 minutes at noon for a walk, and that she would leave her work at the office unless she had a specific deadline to meet that required bringing work home.

Barbara learned to focus on the task or the person at hand and not to be distracted by her long list of things yet to do. She was able to engage with her clients and colleagues and to experience positive emotions about her work and about her clients, all of which reduced her stress level dramatically. Most importantly, Barbara finally reconnected with why she was doing her work. She had started her practice because she enjoyed the substantive work and felt that she was making a positive contribution, but somewhere along the way she started doing so much that she lost sight of her motivations. Instead of feeling only the grind of her practice, Barbara now reconnected with the joy and sense of service.

After we worked together, Barbara was able to get more done while she was at work and to enjoy her time away from the office. She had a much more settled, focused staff. Her clients felt that they had her full attention. Her husband felt she was truly present when she was at home, leaving work worries behind and spending quality time together instead. Because she connected more deeply with clients and others who could send clients her

way, Barbara received more referrals. She also lost about 20 pounds, which helped to increase her physical energy and her positive outlook. In our last conversation she told me, "This has been a very different approach to practice, and I was skeptical at first! Now I know that if I do the things that I've been doing, I can keep going and I can continue this practice. I enjoy it much more, I feel much better, and I am much better at it." Barbara is a particularly good example of what I have seen numerous clients experience after applying the First Foundation of Time Mastery.

For Further Reading

The foregoing description of energy management is intended to be an overview to kick-start your process of refining your self-management. It only scratches the surface, however. For additional information and to build on how to use the capacities and other tools to maximize your energy and performance, see the resources on page 129 by Tony Schwartz and Jim Loehr.

Seven Foundations of Time Mastery for Attorneys

Chapter Five

Foundation 2: Set Priorities and Act Accordingly

To apply the Second Foundation of Time Mastery, you must set priorities for your work and then use those priorities to guide your actions every day. Setting your "to do" list according to your priorities means that you have a guiding plan for each day as well as a sense of what matters most. Knowing your top priorities each day increases the likelihood that you will accomplish (or at least advance) the most important tasks each day.

You will also handle interruptions effectively because you will have a clearer sense of which interruptions actually deserve your attention. Most lawyers have frequent interruptions—emails, telephone calls, and drop–in visits, among others. Setting priorities will help you to know what to do when one of those interruptions arises. Do you need to drop everything and turn your attention to the interruption? Or is the interruption best handled by planning a time to deal with it later and continuing with your current

> Knowing your top priorities each day increases the likelihood that you will accomplish (or advance) the most important tasks each day.

Seven Foundations of Time Mastery for Attorneys

activity? Your priorities will provide the answer.

Successful prioritization requires four steps:

1. Capture all of the tasks you must accomplish.
2. Assign a priority to each task.
3. Devise a plan to handle each task according to its priority status.
4. Execute that plan effectively.

Step One: Create a Master To–Do List

Create a master to–do list that includes all of the tasks you need to complete, both work-related and personal. You may be surprised by the recommendation to combine work and personal tasks, but most lawyers find that merging work and personal tasks in a single location is more effective than separating them. After all, you must ensure that both business and personal tasks are completed, and knowing the status of both at the same time will allow you to use your time well. Creating a single master task list also helps to reduce the common problem of worrying about personal matters while you should be working and worrying about work matters while you could be enjoying free time.

> **Create a master to–do list that includes all of the tasks you need to complete, both work-related and personal. Remember—all "open loops" must be captured.**

If you feel that you are losing track of all that you need to do, read *Getting Things Done: The Art of Stress–Free Productivity*, by David Allen, a classic text on time management and organization. One of the principles Allen sets forth is that all "open loops" must be captured. Open loops are the tasks that must be completed before a project or communication is concluded. Imagine that you are lying in bed, about to fall asleep and a thought pops into your head: *Did I send the letter? Did I answer the email?* That's an open loop. The thoughts that pop into your head while you are relaxing or driving are examples of open loops that you may forget if you do not have a system to capture them.

What open loops are floating around in your head? Write down everything that occurs to you here, and then flag this page (and any addendum pages you may need) for future reference. If this assignment feels overwhelming, choose one project and limit your list to its open loops.

_____
_____
_____
_____
_____
_____
_____
_____

Capture *all* of your open loops in a single master document, and make it a habit to transfer notes about your open loops into that document on a daily basis. I suggest you use a computer system (as simple as a word processing file or as complex as you like) so you can keep track of each item and sort your list into categories. The more you can get out of your mind onto paper, the more effective you will be and the fewer things you'll forget. Review this sample master task list (with a priority column to be completed in Step Two):

Project	Task	Category	Due Date	Priority
Smith v. Jones	Draft discovery plan	Cases	2/1/12	
Complete CLE		Administrative	12/31/11	
Vacation	Plan dates	Personal	11/7/11	

As you see, the project is the case or matter name, the task (if a single task), or the overall goal. The task is the step that must be completed, and most projects will include multiple tasks. Tasks should be bite–sized. If a task can be broken down into a smaller component, it probably should be. Listing only discrete tasks (rather than multi–step tasks or projects that include several tasks) helps to ensure that no open loop escapes your list.

Create a limited list of fairly broad categories for your master task list. The purpose of the categories is to allow you to sort them into meaningful lists and see, for example, all of the case or matter items on your list, all of the personal items, and so on. Categories lose their usefulness if too specific.

Note that many online task management systems now exist and that each offers specific advantages and disadvantages. If you are considering using one of those systems, please visit the Seven Foundations resource website (www.SevenFoundations.com) for suggestions on how to select the right system for you.

> **Listing only discrete tasks (rather than multi–step tasks or projects that include several tasks) helps to ensure that no open loop escapes your list.**

 **Develop your own Master List. Begin a word processing file for this purpose, set up a task list in Outlook, or create whatever system will be most effective for you. Do this now, before you continue to Step Two.**

Step Two: Prioritize

Prioritization is the foundation for accomplishing the time mastery goal of doing the right things at the right time. By setting priorities, you define what tasks must be done when or which tasks take precedence over others. Be aware that you will likely need to reprioritize your to–do list on a frequent basis: as circumstances change, priorities also change. Even amid changing circumstances, however, setting priorities will provide guidance, especially if you use a flexible approach as described here.

Bob wanted to make some changes in his practice. He did not hire me to work specifically on time management, but as we were talking, I noticed that he was constantly on the go, in the office for as many as 14 hours every day, and feeling as if he would never get through his work. Bob complained about the amount of time he spent in the office as compared to the number of hours he was able to bill and told me he didn't understand why he was so busy and yet so unproductive.

I noticed that Bob spent a tremendous amount of time organizing and re–organizing files and papers, non–billable work that made him feel better but was often unnecessary. On reflection, Bob realized that he was organizing so he could have everything laid out in "perfect" order before he started his billable work. He concluded that his files were generally in good enough order and that spending time to make their organization perfect was a poor use of his time. After examining his files and considering his personal preferences, Bob was able to identify the point of diminishing returns for organizing, which helped him to determine when organizing would (and would not) be a priority. He also identified several other ways in which he was engaging in ineffective busywork, and he committed to making changes.

By implementing the Four Quadrant System (presented in the next section), Bob became much clearer about how to determine which tasks were priorities and which were not, and he became determined to act according to the priorities he set. Ending the unnecessary organizing was a big step for Bob, and he resolved to live with adequate organization and to give up shuffling papers in an effort to reach perfection.

Several months after we had completed our work, Bob called to let me know about the positive changes in his practice, and he told me a story about the impact of prioritizing rather than creating black-and-white rules about his desire to be organized. Bob said he had been preparing for a deposition and began by organizing his papers, getting them set out so that he knew where every document was. He stopped himself because he recognized he was engaged in exactly the activity he had decided to avoid. Then he reconsidered, concluding that the organization was important to do in this situation so that he would be able to pull any document at a moment's notice during the deposition. Bob shared, "I had always thought in the past that doing that sort of work was a delay tactic for me, and most of the time it was. But now I see that it can be the right thing to do under some circumstances."

Bob pinpointed and changed a habit that was not working for him. Moreover, he recognized that effectiveness often depends on the circumstances in play and that flexibility would lead to better results than ironclad rules. Although this example demonstrates flexibility in application of techniques for time mastery, the same is true of prioritization. What is immaterial and even wasteful in one setting may become critical in another.

The Four Quadrant Method of Prioritization

One tool makes a bigger difference for my clients than any other: prioritizing according to the Four Quadrant System, based on the work of Stephen Covey (perhaps best known for *The Seven Habits of Highly Effective People*), A. Roger Merrill, and Rebecca Merrill in *First Things First*. The quadrants are represented as follows, with some examples of the activities that fall in each quadrant:

I. Urgent and Important	II. Not Urgent, But Important
• Deadlines, crises, pressing problems • Preparation for today's meeting	• Relationship–building • Planning and strategizing • Preparation for next week's meeting
III. Urgent, Not Important	**IV. Not Urgent, Not Important**
• Interruptions • Some phone calls (e.g. telemarketers) • Some meetings	• Junk mail • Chatting about a celebrity's latest escapade • Trivia and busy work

The metrics for this system of prioritizing are "urgent" and "important." We all know what *urgent* means—it is something that needs to be addressed immediately or the opportunity will pass. A ringing telephone is urgent: you must answer it or you will miss that call. A court hearing is urgent because failing to attend and to be there on time may compromise your client's interests and even your reputation or freedom. *Important* refers to something that is of great consequence, significance, or value. The juxtaposition of urgent and important (or the absence of either) determines the priority of each quadrant, as explained below.

Quadrant I encompasses tasks that are both urgent and important. Most of us live in Quadrant I most of the time: putting out fires, completing deadline–based tasks, drafting a brief shortly before the deadline, getting ready for a closing that will take place the next day, or preparing for a client meeting that will take place in the next 20 minutes. In Quadrant I, activity

Seven Foundations of Time Mastery for Attorneys

means doing important things under urgent circumstances. Learn to recognize Quadrant I activities as important tasks that are coming up with an imminent deadline looming.

> **Quadrant I encompasses tasks that are both urgent and important. The key question, is, how much of your work *must* fall into Quadrant I?**

Quadrant I tends to be the high–stress quadrant. When working on an urgent timeline, stress levels tend to rise. You have less time for reflection and revision. You are trying to get important things done on a short deadline, and this style of activity is a sure recipe for stress.

You will spend some time in Quadrant I while practicing law. The key is to minimize your Quadrant I time.

We all know that doing a task shortly before a deadline can be, in some circumstances, effective. (This may be particularly true in the litigation context, since shifting deadlines can invalidate work done too far in advance.) Working under a looming deadline is sometimes absolutely necessary. The key question, however, is how much of your work *must* fall into Quadrant I? You will likely find that the less work you do under pressure, the more effective and less stressed you will be.

You may need to live in Quadrant I during an entire day on occasion, and you will find that those days are typically your most stressful. As you learn to prioritize according to the Four Quadrant System, though, you will begin to identify and work on important tasks before they become urgent, thus reducing your time in Quadrant I and moving more and more tasks into Quadrant II.

Quadrant II includes tasks that are important, but not urgent. Examples include strategizing and laying plans for an event or deadline that is not imminent. For litigators, an example would be developing the theme of your

Seven Foundations of Time Mastery for Attorneys

case in its early stages or working on a motion for summary judgment several weeks before the deadline for filing. Tax lawyers might envision a Quadrant II activity as working with a client on a thorny tax issue months before the deadline to file the return.

Working in Quadrant II tends to reduce stress, and the work produced in Quadrant II tends to be of higher quality because you have the opportunity to think through the work more deliberately and with less pressure. You also have the time for detailed proofreading after letting a document sit and get "cold" for a few days, as well as the opportunity to rework an entire document if you find it necessary to do so.

One client told me about a heart-stopping experience: he read a "rush job" brief after it had been filed, and he was horrified to see a parenthetical in the factual statement that read, "Is this really true???" Mistakes happen, but they are much less likely when operating in Quadrant II. The more Quadrant II work you can do, the less Quadrant I work will be necessary, simply because you get the bulk of the work done before it becomes an urgent, high-stress, do-or-die scenario.

> **Quadrant II includes tasks that are important, but not urgent. Maximize your Quadrant II time to maximize your effectiveness.**

Renewing energy (physical, emotional, mental, and purposeful) fits into Quadrant II as well. Activities that let you recover energy are "true recreation:" they promote re-creation of energy. We all know from experience that resting and relaxing usually are not urgent: under sufficient pressure, it is possible to push through physical, mental, and emotional exhaustion, and we can function with low-grade fatigue for months or even years. However, we also know that we perform better and feel better when we have had an opportunity to rest, relax, and do something pleasurable. These activities fall into Quadrant II, and performing them on a non-urgent basis avoids the burnout or physical crisis that requires urgent recovery.

The Scottish have a saying: "that which can be done at any time will be done at no time." If you have ever caught yourself showing a guest around your hometown and noticing that you never go to see the sights any other time, you have experienced the truth of that maxim. When something is too convenient, we tend to delay and delay: it ceases to matter if we do the thing today because we could so easily do it tomorrow.

Quadrant II operates under the same principle. Most Quadrant II activities can be done at any time, or in some instances (such as planning your career and setting professional goals), they can be skipped entirely without obvious consequences. Consequences do, of course, exist, but they may remain hidden, causing a career to corrode unseen. If you do not intentionally carve out time to take care of Quadrant II tasks, they may go undone, or they will get done under the stress and pressure of Quadrant I—probably with concomitant consequences.

Finally, clients appreciate lawyers who work in Quadrant II. All too often, lawyers send important documents to their clients and request a fast response. That practice is disrespectful of the client's time. It creates the impression that the lawyer simply could not get his act together in time to plan in advance and complete the work early enough to allow the client time for meaningful review. Clients appreciate lawyers who handle matters during an emergency, but they tend to resent those who act as if every event is an emergency. Living in Quadrant II will increase the quality of your client service.

Maximize your Quadrant II time to maximize your effectiveness.

> **Quadrant III includes tasks and activities that are urgent but not important, many of which can be minimized.**

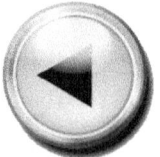

Seven Foundations of Time Mastery for Attorneys

Quadrant III includes tasks and activities that are urgent but not important. Some Quadrant III activities are immediately recognizable, such as a meeting you must attend that never produces results. You might imagine Quadrant III as a triage space: many activities are initially slotted in Quadrant III because they are urgent, and only by addressing them will you discover whether they are also important and thus resident in Quadrant I. For instance, a ringing telephone is urgent. It could be a telemarketer or it could be someone calling with the biggest case of your career. You will not know until you take the call.

Everyone will spend time in Quadrant III because of required activities (such as completing mandatory but useless paperwork), and time is needed to assess whether a task is important. The key is to recognize when you are in Quadrant III and to minimize that time.

> Quadrant IV encompasses tasks and activities that are neither urgent nor important; these tasks are best eliminated.

Quadrant IV encompasses tasks and activities that are neither urgent nor important. Sitting slumped in front of the TV at the end of a long day and mindlessly watching whatever you find on the screen simply because you are too tired to do anything else is a Quadrant IV activity. It does not renew your energy (in fact, it may further deplete it), so channel–surfing is not important, and it certainly is not urgent. It is simply wasted time. Compare that with watching a television show you truly enjoy, one that makes you laugh or think. After watching such a show, your energy level will increase because you enjoyed the time and you got pleasure from it. Increasing your energy through recreation indicates a Quadrant II activity.

Typically, we can recognize Quadrant IV activities in advance, because we know what is a pure waste of time. Most of us fall into Quadrant IV activity (especially mindless television or web surfing) simply because the

activity is lulling and may even be pleasant, though not truly pleasurable. The more attention you pay to what refreshes you as opposed to what leaves you feeling drained or bored, the less time you will spend in Quadrant IV.

You will, however, spend *some* time in Quadrant IV. Everyone does. But because the time spent in Quadrant IV is unproductive, you will not feel better or do better as a result of spending time there. Notice when you are engaged in a Quadrant IV activity and choose to do something different, even if that means taking a nap instead of engaging in passive, meaningless activity.

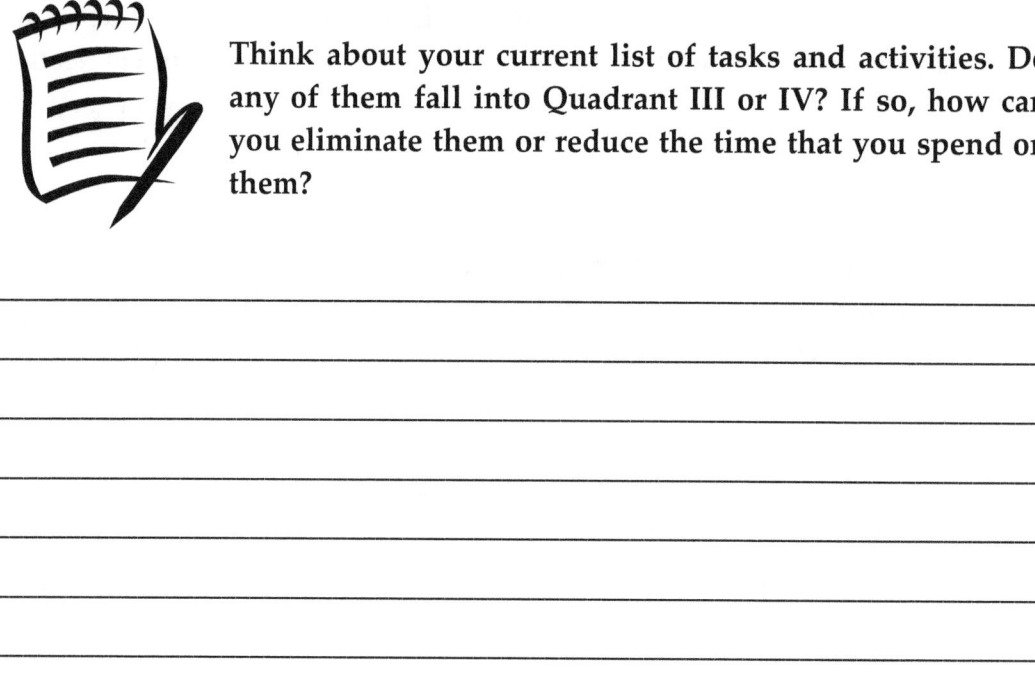

Think about your current list of tasks and activities. Do any of them fall into Quadrant III or IV? If so, how can you eliminate them or reduce the time that you spend on them?

___

Return to the Master Task List you created at the end of Step One, and use the Quadrants to assign a priority to each task. Consider using the Quadrant numbers (1–4) for easy computer sorting.

Step Three: Devise a Plan to Accomplish Your Tasks

Now that you have a prioritized master task list, break it down into weekly action lists. Look first to your Quadrant I tasks, and put them on this week's list. (If your immediate reaction is that not all of them need to be accomplished this week, you have probably included some non-urgent activities that should be placed in Quadrant II instead.) Then evaluate your Quadrant II activities and determine which should be addressed this week. Think critically: your goal is to prevent any Quadrant II activity from becoming a Quadrant I activity. This goal is likely to be somewhat unrealistic initially, simply because you will probably need to clear the decks of urgent tasks before you can move into significant Quadrant II time. The sooner you can get to Quadrant II, activities, however, the sooner you will change the way you spend your time.

 **Create your Weekly Action List. As with the Master List, maintaining the weekly list on your computer may be most effective for easy sorting. Note that you will do this step weekly, preferably at the end of each week.**

Now, plan the necessary actions to accomplish each task on your Weekly Action List. What can you delegate, and what must you do yourself? Make notes on both the Weekly Action List and the Master List so that you know at a glance the status of every item on your lists. (See Foundation Three for delegation best practices.)

Finally, each evening, refer to your Weekly Action List to create your Daily To Do List for the next day. Again, make sure that the list is organized by priority so you know what your first task is each day. One benefit of this approach is that having a prioritized list of tasks to accomplish every day will make it easier for you to begin working on your top priority each morning without even needing to pause and consider what that top priority is.

Nevertheless, earlybirds may prefer to create this list on arriving in the office each morning. Whenever you create your Daily To Do List, having the list to guide your daily approach will help you to use your time more effectively, and you will reap the maximum benefit from your early morning energy.

Create your Daily To Do List for tomorrow. I suggest you keep this list on a small piece of paper (I recommend a 4" x 6" Post–It® note for easy visibility) so that you do not get carried away and list an unattainable number of tasks to accomplish each day. However you choose to keep your list, be sure you put it somewhere you will see throughout the day to help you stay on track.

Step Four: Execute Your Plan Effectively

Having identified and prioritized your tasks and devised a plan to accomplish the necessary tasks today and this week, the final step is to execute your plan effectively. This step incorporates several time mastery habits that allow you to make the best possible use of your time.

Multi–Tasking: Don't Do It.

Perhaps you have heard the recently–coined word "frazzing," which means frantic multi-tasking. That describes how many of us operate throughout the day. Although many lawyers believe that multi–tasking is an effective way to use time, the evidence indicates otherwise.

Neurobiological evidence shows that although we think we can do two things at once, we are only kidding ourselves, unless both activities can be performed without thought, like walking and chewing gum. When both activities require thought or judgment, they cannot be performed

simultaneously. For instance, suppose you are talking on a cell phone while driving. You can do both while driving on "autopilot." If someone turns in front of you, however, you will need to pay attention to either the driving or the conversation: you will find it impossible to do both at the same time. The brain is not capable of doing two *processing* activities at the same time, and when it tries, it creates a bottleneck. Sometimes that bottleneck is so tiny we fail to notice it, but it exists nonetheless. If you are driving while talking and you need to concentrate on the driving, without making a conscious decision, you will stop talking until you can return to managing both.

One common attempt at multi-tasking is reading email while talking to someone on the telephone or in person. Before deciding that is an effective use of your time, consider a 2005 study conducted for Hewlett-Packard through the Institute of Psychiatry at the University of London. The study found that, "Workers distracted by e-mail and phone calls suffer a fall in IQ more than twice that found in marijuana smokers." The study concluded that distractions due to responding to incoming emails, text messages, and phone calls caused a temporary 10-point drop in IQ, which is equivalent to the "brain fog" you might experience if you were to miss an entire night of sleep.

Multi-tasking is not a badge of honor. Multi-tasking *costs* time and cripples effectiveness. It splits your focus. The brain is simply not able to handle two processing tasks at once, no matter how much we would like to believe otherwise.

> **Multi-tasking *costs* time and cripples effectiveness.**

My client Rhonda told me that she used her time very effectively, more so than most people. One of her habits was reading her email while taking telephone calls. I told her about the 2005 study, and she told me that while others might suffer from multi-tasking, she excelled at it. Undaunted, I let the point drop for the moment. Toward the end of our telephone

conversation, I noticed that Rhonda was still responding to me and remaining on point, but that her speech had slowed down and she was saying "ummm" and "ahhh" much more than she had at the beginning of our call. I inquired whether there was any chance she was looking at her email, and Rhonda was astonished. She asked how I could possibly tell, and then after a sheepish laugh, admitted that perhaps she was not the multi-tasking master she had believed. Of course, we have all been on the receiving end of someone else's distraction. Most of us think we are much better at fooling other people than we really are. Rhonda quit her email multi-tasking and found that, as a result, she built more genuine relationships and used her time more efficiently.

When are you most likely to multi-task? If you are unsure, ask your assistant what he or she has noticed. Evaluate the effectiveness of your multi-tasking. (Remember, some multi-tasking can be quite effective when one task requires no mental processing, such as reading during a train ride to or from your office.)

_____
_____
_____
_____
_____
_____
_____
_____

Use the Quadrants to Manage Interruptions

When you have an interruption, pause to figure out which Quadrant it represents. An interruption is by definition urgent, so ask whether it is important. If it not, it is a Quadrant III event and it probably does not merit disrupting what you are doing to handle it. (The exception, of course, is when the interruption carries some hierarchical overtones, such as those in play when a partner interrupts a junior associate working for her to do something that is "not important." Absent unusual circumstances, the associate will want to meet the partner's request even if the activity would otherwise fall into Quadrant III.) A Quadrant I interruption will likely require immediate attention.

If you determine that an interruption is in Quadrant III—perhaps your assistant is eager to tell you about something non-work-related, or maybe you have received a call from a college friend who just wants to catch up—defer the interruption and return to the task at hand. Politely but firmly tell the person who is interrupting you that you are wrapped up in something else right now and set a time to reconvene. At that point, the interruption loses its urgency, and you can decide either to handle it as a Quadrant II activity (important, but lacking urgency) or you can discover that it is a Quadrant IV activity (neither urgent nor important) and choose not to handle it at all.

Think about the last interruption you remember. Using the Quadrants, how would you characterize it, and how would you respond now?

_____

_____

_____

Recovering from Interruptions

Whether you determine that an interruption does justify switching your focus or whether you conclude that you should stay on task and return to the interruption at a later time, dealing with an interruption incurs a cost. Knowing how to minimize that cost can prevent an interruption from becoming a rupture in your productivity. A study by researchers at the University of California at Irvine found that workers are interrupted, on average, every three minutes. Following an interruption, workers required about 23 minutes to get back to the original task, typically cycling through two other tasks in the interim. About 20% of the time, the worker did not return to the original task on the same day. The study proves what we all know intuitively: when work is interrupted, whether by a telephone call, the beep that announces you have received a new email, or by someone who stops by the office, effectiveness drops dramatically.

When you are interrupted, try these tips to bring yourself back to your work as quickly as possible.

- *If you are writing, stop in the middle of a thought.* If you finish your thought, shift your attention to the interruption, and then try to pick up where you left off, you have no breadcrumb trail to lead you back into your thought process. If you stop in the middle of a sentence or in the middle of a thought, however, the dangling work serves as a prompt you can use on your return. Picking up a thought already in process gives you a toehold you can use to complete your thought and then continue on.
- Use Post–It® flags or a red pen to *mark your place* in reading or writing.
- Write a few words to *capture your train of thought* and cue your memory.
- Make it your habit to *return to your work immediately following an interruption.* Stick to your planned work and do not allow yourself to shift your focus to a new activity.

- Don't hesitate to *let the person who is interrupting with a visit or telephone call know that you are busy*. Be polite, but focus on the interruption and do not slide into chit–chat. The quicker you can deal with the interruption, the quicker you can return to your work, and the more likely that you will actually do so.

 Which tactics are most helpful to you in making sure you do not lose your train of thought because of an interruption? What habits can you use to ensure that you return to the task at hand following an interruption?

_____
_____
_____
_____

Block Your Time

The best way to manage interruptions, of course, is to prevent them (to the extent possible) from occurring. Time blocking offers an ideal opportunity to focus your efforts on one task at a time in a concentrated manner, while limiting interruptions.

Create quiet hours for yourself when you will not be disturbed and can work with concentration and focus. I recommend that you set aside the first two to three hours in the morning for this focused time and let your assistant and colleagues know that this is your sacred work time. (If you are not a morning person, try shifting this quiet time to the end of the day, especially if your office tends to be less busy late in the day.) Unless a client calls with a true emergency, unless the court calls, unless a child or spouse calls with a crisis, you should not be interrupted.

> **Studies show that between 45 minutes and 90 minutes is the optimal amount of time for concentrated attention to work.**

Time may be required to train your assistant and colleagues in what is truly an emergency. Be ruthless in protecting your time: if you fail to enforce that boundary, you will never get the uninterrupted time you need. Studies show that between 45 minutes and 90 minutes is the optimal amount of time for concentrated attention to work. If you set aside an hour or two hours for focused work on your top task, you will be much more effective—particularly if you do so when your energy is at its natural peak.

Batch similar tasks. Create blocks of time in which you can work on like tasks. For example, you might experiment with handling your correspondence in a block or focusing on a particular case or client during one block. Once you get up to speed on doing a task, it makes sense to keep rolling with it rather than shifting tasks and getting up to speed again. Grouping like tasks also allows your brain to get into a groove so that you can move through the tasks more quickly, with less mental switching time required.

In addition, creating blocks of time in which you are available for appointments or to return telephone calls means that your assistant will not need to interrupt you to find out when you would like to talk with someone. You will train clients and colleagues to know when you will be available, thus managing their expectations about when they can expect an opportunity to speak with you. By letting others know in advance when you will be available to talk with them for routine matters, you will eliminate numerous interruptions.

What blocks of time would be helpful for you to create? Use this space to identify the hours you will set aside for your concentrated work, and list the tasks that you can combine during specific blocks of time.

Chapter Six

Foundation 3: Delegate Effectively

The Third Foundation of Time Mastery is effective delegation. Delegation is an assumed competency for lawyers: if you ask any lawyer whether she is a good delegator, without much thought most lawyers would probably answer, "yes," or at least, "I'm good enough." Given a little more thought, though, most lawyers can remember too many times when a delegated project has gone askew, revealing miscommunication, insufficient direction, or an incomplete understanding of the project. These problems are often the consequence of poor delegation skills.

A number of clients have told me that they want to delegate and that bright support staff and colleagues are eager to take on additional work. For some reason, though, they find that delegated projects go wrong, and the delegators generally blame those doing the work for a lack of understanding. The truth is that both parties could likely stand to improve on giving and receiving projects.

In fact, most lawyers are only passably adequate at delegating work. Delegation goes well enough that, despite frequent frustration, there is little impetus to work to become excellent. The gap between adequate and excellent delegation skills is wide, however, and may be measured in lost

Seven Foundations of Time Mastery for Attorneys

minutes (the billable time required to explain, again, what is needed for a project), in lost hours (when a project comes in and is not correct, so you have to take over the work or reassign it, and you cannot bill the client for all of the hours spent on the project), and in lost dollars.

> **The gap between adequate and excellent delegation skills is wide, and may be measured in lost minutes, in lost hours, and in lost dollars.**

Lawyers often tend to rush through delegation, thinking more about the time savings that delegating generates and the perfect product that will emerge from the delegate's work than about the directions and information that will reap those rewards. Saving time and receiving an excellent work product requires delegating well and identifying which activities can and should be delegated—and which cannot or should not. Poor delegation takes more time than it could ever save, so you must learn to delegate effectively.

Effective delegation is critical to getting what you need, when you need it, in the form that you need it, and thus to saving yourself time. Depending on the task you have delegated, you may need to do some additional work to massage the product you receive into final form. If you have delegated well, though, you will not need to start over completely. Reaching that level of skill requires practice and forethought.

The Top Five Mistakes in Delegating Work

The top five delegation mistakes are rushing, delegating too little, delegating too much, micromanaging, and not managing enough.

1. **Rushing.** Making an assignment before thinking about the key aspects of delegation (set forth in the next section) is almost a guarantee that you will not get the end result that you want. Without

sitting down to think about what the finished product should be, you may not even know what you really need. As a result you will not clearly communicate information about your true need while making the assignment. Rushing means that you may not select the best person to whom to delegate the task, or that you may fail to describe exactly what you need to know and/or how you want the final product delivered.

When you rush to delegate a project, you likely will not get what you need and want. You will end up frustrated and having lost time rather than saved it: not only do you have to do the work yourself (or re-delegate it), but you are likely bumping into a deadline because of the wasted time, landing your task squarely in Quadrant I, with all of the associated stress.

> **When you rush to delegate a project, you likely will end up frustrated and having lost time rather than saved it.**

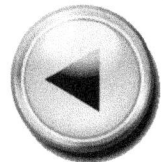

An example: Paula, a partner, asked Evan, a third-year associate, to draft a deposition outline. She told Evan that she did not want the outline to include questions, and that instead she wanted a subject matter outline. Evan took Paula's direction literally and prepared an extensive outline organized by topic, with issues set out below each topic and supported by well-organized, highlighted, and flagged documents.

Paula was livid, however, when she discovered that the outline did not include questions. She had wanted Evan to skip the opening questions but to include questions that would get to the heart of the factual and legal issues—but because she said, "no questions," Evan misunderstood. Should he have clarified before completing the outline? Absolutely. Paula, however, bears responsibility as well for a problem that could have been avoided had she simply paused to think about how best to describe the work product that she wanted to receive.

2. **Delegating too little.** Lawyers are highly skilled and self–reliant, and too many of us believe that we should be in control of every aspect of our practices. But here is some news: you do not need to be a lone ranger. Failing to delegate costs you time. Moreover, if you do not give your staff and junior colleagues stretch projects that challenge and engage them, they will not advance professionally. Instead, they will get bored and probably move on to another position, or worse yet you will find yourself surrounded by "zombies" who show up to the office everyday but are completely disengaged from their work.

3. **Delegating too much.** The first problem with over–delegating is, of course, that it presents numerous ethical issues. You cannot delegate legal work to non–lawyers without adequate supervision, and you should not delegate legal work to other lawyers without appropriate supervision.

   Even when you are delegating administrative tasks only, over–delegation results in poor practice management. You should not perform the day–to–day administrative tasks required for your practice, but you must be able to do so if you find yourself short–staffed. This does not mean that you should be as skilled as your assistants at everything from filing to document formatting to mail room procedures, but you should know enough to muddle your way through when necessary.

4. **Micromanaging.** Micromanaging produces problems similar to those encountered with under–delegating, though the problems arise even more quickly and tend to be more acute. Micromanagement undermines the confidence and/or morale of the person to whom you have delegated a project because it sends the message that you do not trust his judgment. That person may leave or become a zombie as previously described, but more likely he will become frustrated and resentful. Micromanagers often have a reputation as

being impossible to please, and those who cannot be pleased often find that those who work with them quit trying.

Equally troublesome, micromanagement prevents the person doing the work from exercising her own judgment and expanding her professional development. Those who are micromanaged lack the opportunity to bring their perspectives and ideas to the table, which means that the micromanager loses the chance to be wowed by what those who have been assigned the work could do if only they had sufficient freedom.

5. **Not managing enough.** Failure to manage adequately can produce the same problems that rushing and over-delegation can produce. You may encounter ethical issues that could have been avoided with proper supervision, and you may not receive the work product that you wanted and expected.

Do you recognize your habits in any of these top mistakes? If so, note them here so that you can change your approach to delegation in the future, using the suggestions that follow.

_____
_____
_____
_____
_____

Avoid the Mistakes and Becoming an Excellent Delegator

Fortunately, learning to become an excellent delegator requires only two habits: forethought and repetition. Think through the key aspects of any assignment and delegate using the answers to six classic questions: Who, what, when, where, how, and why?

Who has the skills necessary to complete this assignment? To whom can you make the assignment, and to whom should you? Consider not only who is more capable, but also how taking on the assignment at issue will affect the candidates' professional development. Depending on the task at issue, if a potential delegate has been doing the task flawlessly for an extended period of time, perhaps the time has come to give him a more challenging assignment and to pass the task on to someone else.

What needs to be done, precisely? What work product do you want to receive? Describe your desired outcome in detail. For example, a research assignment can be designed to find the line of cases that sets out the legal answer to your question, or it can be geared to find the one case that allows you to make a creative argument on which the courts have not yet ruled. Likewise, you may or may not want to explore related issues that come up in the course of research, and you may or may not want someone to draft supporting documents for the project you've assigned. Finally, you might want an oral "quick and dirty" response, an email explanation, or a full memorandum with attachments that you can provide to the client or the court. Phrasing the assignment and the desired result clearly will ensure that the person doing the work knows what you want to receive.

> **When delegating, specify the deadline and confirm that the person doing the work expects to be able to meet the deadline.**

When is the deadline? One of the key problems in making assignments is the temptation to resort to a non–specific deadline. "Friday" is not an adequate statement of the deadline unless Friday at 11:59 P.M. is acceptable to you. By the same token, "ASAP" is subject to so many different interpretations that it is best avoided. You may take "ASAP" to mean, *drop everything to handle this project and get the result to me as soon as humanly*

possible even if it means staying up for three days to do so. The person to whom you are delegating the project may genuinely understand ASAP to mean, *please start this as soon as you can and get it to me as soon as you can, but I don't expect you to drop everything or even to skip lunch to get it done.* If you mean the former and the person handling the project assumes the latter, the result will be frustrating, if not catastrophic.

Instead, specify the deadline ("Wednesday no later than 3 P.M.") and confirm that the person doing the work expects to be able to meet the deadline you set. If the project is particularly time-sensitive, be sure to convey that fact. Although you can assume that your delegate will endeavor to meet your deadline, if your project is one that would be crippled by any delay, you should say so upfront. Otherwise, your delegate may assume, incorrectly, that a *de minimis* delay would be acceptable.

Where and How should the project be completed? *Where* is generally less important than *how*, though if you know that research must start in the library rather than online, be sure to mention that, especially to newer lawyers. (You may, in fact, even need to acquaint the new lawyer with where to find a law library.) When you describe how the assignment should be completed, tread carefully to avoid the risks of micromanagement and insufficient management, and consider the experience level of the person completing the work when you make the assignment.

> **Thinking through the delegation questions in advance increases the likelihood that you will receive the product you want when you need it.**

When you consider how a project should be completed, decide whether any special circumstances exist. Would you like interim research results to be summarized in a table? Do you want that table to be generated as a Word document, or would you prefer Excel? The "how" piece generally covers the workproduct that precedes the final product you will receive. So, for instance, if you have requested a memorandum with supporting cases in the order each is mentioned in the memorandum, with the cases' holding highlighted, consider whether you will want the highlighting to show up on photocopies. If yes, part of the "how" will be that your delegate should use a blue or pink highlighter; if not, he should use yellow. After a delegate has performed that kind of project once, he will know what to do, but describing that "how" upfront during the first assignment will save significant frustration for both of you.

Why is this work necessary? Sometimes providing context and background to orient the person doing the work as to how the project fits into the larger picture is beneficial. Context and factual issues may change everything from strategy to the answer to a specific research question. Providing the background is not always necessary, but consider doing so in each assignment so that you will be sure to include the extra information when it is necessary.

Thinking through each of these aspects of an assignment increases the chances that you will get the work product that you want, when you want it. Until you have developed a strong working relationship with someone to whom you assign work, you might also consider two additional steps to ensure that she understood the assignment correctly and that the project is going according to plan.

First, *ask the person to restate, using her own words, what she understands the assignment to be* and what kind of work product she expects to produce. Consider how you phrase this request: "let's be sure we're on the same page" sets an entirely different tone from, "I want to be sure you understand what I want."

Second, *ask the person doing the work to check in with you* a few days into the project. You will have an opportunity to be sure that the work is going in the right direction and to clear up any questions. Note that saying, "check with me if you have any problems" is not sufficient to accomplish this. Instead, arrange a time (even if it's just a specific morning or afternoon) for a short conversation.

 Seven Foundations of Time Mastery for Attorneys

Identify Tasks to Delegate

Some delegable tasks are obvious: research, initial drafting of a document, and filing are common examples. However, you can create systems that allow for delegation where it would otherwise be difficult to do so.

Notice what tasks you do repeatedly and consider how you might create a system to make the task routine. (You may find it helpful to keep a sheet of paper or an open document to record the tasks you find yourself doing more than once or twice.) Having created a system, look to see whether some or all of it can be delegated.

For example, you might prefer to open your mail and to separate it into folders for each client, for CLE, for bar-related activities, and so on. That task is easily delegated, as soon as you can identify what categories to use for the sorting and how you would like the files arranged.

If you have applied the time-blocking technique previously recommended, you have probably set up certain hours for client appointments and telephone calls. That leads to easy delegation because your assistant need not ask when you would like to schedule a call or meeting, and you need not specify when you would like the appointments to be placed, absent special circumstances.

> **Notice what tasks you do repeatedly and consider how you might create a system to make the task routine. Having created a system, look to see whether some or all of it can be delegated.**

You might also devise a system so that your assistant and more junior lawyers assigned to a particular client matter know to begin working on a project as soon as it arises. For instance, you might ask your assistant to calendar the due date for incoming discovery requests and to direct the requests to a lawyer assigned to the case for initial responses. You will be aware that the requests have been received (perhaps the system will include sending the requests to the junior lawyer by email, with a copy to you) but the junior lawyer will know without question that she should begin drafting. (If you are the junior lawyer on a case, you might even suggest this system, since it will streamline the work and remove one task from the senior lawyer's list of things to do. Suggestions that make a more senior lawyer's life easier are almost always welcome.)

Finally, you likely know the importance of staying abreast of your clients' industries and the business developments likely to impact your clients. (This is, in fact, a key way to deliver exceptional client service and to build new business.) Scanning industry newsletters and business news for information germane to your clients can be time–consuming. However, once you have identified the relevant industries and search terms, you can use assistants or Google alerts to cull down to the key articles you should read.

Once you begin looking at your daily activities with a critical eye, you will begin to discover many tasks that you can delegate. If you find that you are continuing to hold on more of your routine work than you should, and if you have a sharp assistant and/or junior colleague, consider asking him what you could be delegating. You might be surprised what he sees and how much he can handle. Finally, whenever you notice that you are doing something not within your special expertise, question whether you should delegate that task. Document formatting is a perfect example: you can certainly make a document look presentable, but you may take three times as long as your assistant would to do so. You should delegate such a task whenever possible.

Think about the activities that you perform over and over. How can you create a system for those activities, and what might you delegate? Think creatively.

_____

_____

_____

_____

_____

Get Extra Assistance

If you find that you have enough delegable work to keep someone occupied for a few hours a month but not enough to hire an (or another) assistant (or if you'd simply prefer not to incur the expense and commitment of an employee) consider hiring a virtual assistant or an intern.

Virtual assistants ("VAs") are ideal to help with any task that does not require their physical presence. While that restriction may seem limiting at first, you'll quickly recognize that almost anything can be accomplished remotely, even filing—you can mail documents to an assistant, who can return them to you arranged as you have specified. Most routine administrative tasks, such as transcribing dictation, scheduling appointments, and making travel arrangements, can be completed by a VA just as easily as they can by someone sitting in the next office.

To find a VA, look for a clearinghouse organization (such as AssistU or IVAA) that allows you to search for assistants with the kinds of skills you require. You can even find a VA with legal experience or expertise as an executive assistant. Be sure to interview several candidates to ensure that the VA you select has the skills you need, especially if she will deal with your clients and opposing counsel.

Another option for limited extra assistance is to hire an intern from a local college. An intern is a good choice for routine tasks that do not require much knowledge about the law or the operation of a legal practice. You get the double benefit of getting the help you need and acting as a mentor, especially if your intern is considering a legal career. To find an intern, check with local schools or post an advertisement on Craigslist. Be sure that you distinguish whether you are seeking a paid or an unpaid intern. If unpaid, carefully consider whether such a relationship is appropriate under the rules promulgated by the Department of Labor. Audits to determine whether unpaid interns are more accurately classified as employees are increasingly routine. (Audits to classify employees as opposed to independent contractors are likewise on the increase, so consider carefully whether delegating as you plan could be appropriate for a contractor based on the Internal Revenue Service rules.)

Whether you decide to hire a VA or an intern, consider the scope of the position through the lens of your new delegation skills. Who would be a good delegate, and what characteristics matter to you? What will you have this person do, and what skills must he have? When and where will your new delegate need to work? How is the work to be performed? And finally, why are you seeking a delegate? At a minimum, your answer should be that delegating certain tasks will allow you to take on other work that produces an hourly income higher than the rate you will pay your new delegate.

Visit SevenFoundations.com to find a Resource List that includes several entries for finding virtual assistance.

Do you need extra assistance to accomplish the administrative tasks that you could delegate? Note here what tasks you'd like to assign to someone else, as well as what qualifications your delegate must have. And then, commit to searching out a VA or intern (or employee, if appropriate) who can support you.

_____
_____
_____
_____
_____

 Seven Foundations of Time Mastery for Attorneys

Chapter Seven

Foundation 4: Manage Your Physical Environment

The physical environment in which you operate has a significant impact on your effectiveness. Your ability to function well will depend, to some degree, on how well you manage each aspect on your physical environment.

Office Environment

If you're working full-time, chances are good that you spend more hours in your office than in any other room you inhabit. Physical energy can be sapped quickly by suffering through days in an uncomfortable chair, under bad lighting, or where the resources you need are in disarray or inconveniently placed. Simple changes will help you to increase your physical, emotional, mental, and purposeful energy by arranging your office to support you.

 Start by assessing your physical comfort. Is your chair comfortable? Is your office a comfortable temperature? Do you have enough light? Can you easily reach the items that you use most frequently? Take a moment to notice everything about your office that is uncomfortable or annoying and compile the list here. Make a commitment to eliminate each of these items within the next month.

Seven Foundations of Time Mastery for Attorneys

_____
_____
_____
_____
_____

Managing Paper

Even as the practice of law moves more and more to a paperless environment, paper tends to continue to be a significant challenge for lawyers, probably second only to email. Numerous books offer help with paper management, including David Allen's *Getting Things Done*, *Taming the Paper Tiger* by Barbara Hemphill, and *Organizing from the Inside Out* by Julie Morgenstern. If dealing with paper presents a serious challenge to you, purchase one of these books and work through the suggestions presented.

Reducing Paper Clutter

If paper is more of an annoyance than a serious problem, however, consider the following suggestions. To reduce clutter and desktop disorganization, I recommend keeping four shallow boxes or files on your desk, labeled as follows:

1. In–box
2. Out–box
3. Pending
4. To Read

Neither the in–box nor the out–box merit much discussion, except to remind you that the in–box must be emptied regularly—at least daily, and preferably twice a day. The in–box is not intended to hold papers for any

length of time, only to receive them. Using a system adapted from *Getting Things Done*, I recommend that you handle each piece of paper in your in-box only once while disposing of it, using this approach:

Does the paper require action?

1. If not, discard the paper or put it in your out-box for permanent filing.

2. If action is required, consider whether to delegate the task or to do it yourself.

    a. Whichever your answer, determine whether you can do it or delegate it in five minutes or less.

        i. If so, complete it immediately.

        ii. If not, move the paper to your pending folder and move on to the next piece of paper in your in-box.

Your **reading file** is designed to corral the non-time sensitive reading you need to do to stay up on your clients' activities, business developments, and legal news. The file should be emptied on a weekly basis. If you want to get extremely organized, you could consider subfolders for the reading file, to break your reading into advance sheets or other legal updates, client-related reading material, bar association magazines or newsletters, and so on. You might also organize the subfolders based on the prioritization system of Foundation Two: Quadrants I, II, and III. (The subfolder for Quadrant IV is your trash can.) If you go that extra mile, though, be sure to delegate the task to someone else, because creating that level of organization is not the highest or best use of your time.

Schedule a time to read the materials in your reading file, and do that reading away from your office. You might take the file to a café or on a business trip to read in flight. Removing the file from your office creates impetus to finish and discard the papers, whereas you may be tempted to defer your reading or to keep papers unnecessarily if you review the file in your office.

If retaining papers "just in case" is a habit, create a special folder for those papers, date it with month and year, and file it away at the end of each month. One year after you begin this system (note the date in your calendar), go back to the first folder. Have you pulled anything from it? If not, discard it. Continue this system as long as necessary to convince yourself that "just in case" papers are rarely necessary and that you can almost always find the information elsewhere if needed.

> **Reading File:** Schedule a time to read the materials in your reading file, and do that reading away from your office.
>
> **Tickler File:** If you maintain an electronic calendar, create an appointment that reminds you to check your tickler file.

The **pending file** must be cleared on a regular basis, at least every two days. Otherwise, it will become an unruly mixture of papers on which you need to take action, papers that should remind you of something, and possibly even papers that you are not sure how to handle. If you find that you are using the pending file to hold papers to remind you of upcoming events or tasks, transfer them to your tickler file.

A **tickler file** is best arranged as an expandable file folder with multiple manila folders inside: one folder for each month, folders labeled 1–31 for each day of the month, and a folder labeled Future. Each month you move the appropriate folder to the front and place all 31 subfolders behind it to represent the days of that month, and make it part of your morning habit to check your tickler file. If you maintain an electronic calendar, create an appointment that reminds you to check your tickler file.

Suppose you are processing your in–box on March 15. You pick up a piece of paper announcing a CLE program you would like to attend, so you put it in your out–box with a note to your assistant to register you for the program, calendar it, and return the flyer. When the flyer reappears in your in-box, you turn to your tickler file and put it in the folder labeled 15 (or 14, if you need a reminder on the evening before to drive to the CLE location instead of to your office) behind your March folder. If the program were to be held on June 17, you would put the piece of paper in the June folder. At the end of each month, pick up the folder for the next month and disperse the pieces of paper in it according to the day of the month on which each piece of paper becomes relevant. Between March 15 and the end of May, the paper would be safely in the June folder. At the end of May, you would pick up the June folder, find the flyer, and put it into the folder labeled 17. (Better yet, you would delegate the entire process to an assistant!)

> Remember that your assistant is likely skilled in managing paper, so do not hesitate to ask for help in clearing clutter.

A tickler creates an evergreen "pending" folder for you. Although you will likely have dates for CLE programs scheduled on your calendar (and so you could rely on your calendar rather than the tickler to remind you of the upcoming program), you may run across other items that require action on a certain date but not before, such as an announcement of an event that would be perfect for entertaining a client, with the ticket purchase date sometime in the future. A tickler file can be invaluable for keeping track of those papers. The folder labeled Future is useful for papers that are not yet ripe but will be in the distant future, such as an advertisement for a hotel for your dream vacation to Italy. Clear that folder quarterly, or more often if necessary, to avoid turning it into a paper dump.

Remember that your assistant is likely skilled in managing paper, so do not hesitate to ask for help in clearing clutter.

Some readers will be appalled at these Luddite suggestions for handling paper. If you prefer to maintain a paperless office, adapt the foregoing suggestions accordingly. For example, rather than maintaining a paper tickler file, scan papers you will need to handle in the future and calendar a dated reminder.

What strategies do you need to implement to reduce paper clutter in your office? Note them here, and discuss with your assistant what kind of help you need.

_____

_____

_____

_____

Filing Strategies for Paper

After you have processed paper to avoid clutter, you will need to create a filing system to maintain documents that you need to keep for future reference. A filing system must be easy to navigate so you can lay your hands on any document quickly. Your assistant should be the primary person to maintain your files and to pull documents from the files when they are needed, but you must know how the files are organized so that you can find documents if necessary. The files must also be sufficiently well-organized to allow someone else to find a document if both you and your assistant are out of the office.

I recommend keeping case and project files that identify your client, the matter name, the day initiated, and a brief description of what is in the file. Maintain a master list that has all of this information, and indicate whether this is an active or inactive matter and whether the file is in storage. This master list is best maintained on a computer so that you can sort by each

 Seven Foundations of Time Mastery for Attorneys

category, but be sure that it is available at any time to anyone who needs to access it. If your assistant creates the file and saves it on her hard drive (so that no one can accidentally open and overwrite it), you may not be able to access it when she is out of the office. Consider printing a master file list at a regular interval (every week or month, depending on the volume of filings) so that you can access the list at any time.

You may have form agreements, discovery forms, motions that you use as a pattern, and the like. Consider keeping your form files electronically for the increased ease of searching and because you can quickly copy and paste from an electronic form into your new document. Be sure to include your forms on your master list so that you can find them easily. For example, suppose that once upon a time you drafted a license agreement, which you do rarely. Five years later, you may need to draft a similar license agreement. Using the master list, you will be able to lay hands on the files very quickly and remember what you called, it, when it was, and find it. If you just have a file, whether paper or electronic, and it is not indexed on a master list, chances are that locating it will take you longer—and you may not even remember that you have such a document to use as a form.

 What changes do you need to make in your filing system? Be sure to discuss changes with your assistant and ask for his input.

_____

_____

_____

_____

_____

If feasible, you may also consider scanning all documents in your office and storing them in a well-organized document management system. Electronic maintenance of paper is often easier to use (assuming that documents are appropriately tagged and archived) and forces fewer decisions about whether to keep documents. Be certain to have a bulletproof, redundant back-up system for your electronic files. (See SevenFoundations.com for back-up system options and maintenance recommendations.)

Chapter Eight

Foundation 5: Tame the Email Tsunami

Although email is intangible and non–physical, its prevalence makes it appear to be not just physical, but the 800–pound gorilla of modern life. Initially designed as a convenience, email has become a medium for communication that has expanded far beyond the paper communications it was designed to replace.

Email can be incredibly useful, and it can also be a huge drain on energy. Email is at the heart of the information tsunami: so many emails flood in on a daily basis that they create a tidal wave of information to be sorted through and managed. Email is also the top contender for interruptions. As of April 2010, an estimated 294 billion emails were sent each day, for a total of some 90 trillion emails per year. No doubt that the number of emails sent has continued to rise and is even higher today. Handling your emails and knowing how to process them will help you to cut down on the amount of time that you have to spend to go through your share of those nearly 300 billion emails.

Effective email management requires attention to each of the following steps:

- Handling the email you receive
    - ◊ Check your email regularly

- Use filters to reduce email in your in-box
- Batch your email review
- Eliminate undesired email
- Sending email
  - Decide whether to send an email
  - Address and name email recipients
  - Use a descriptive subject line
  - Limit the content of the email
  - Ask questions clearly
  - Reply to email
- Retaining email messages
- Reaching "In-Box Empty"

Email can be one of the fastest drains on energy simply because seeing hundreds or even thousands of emails can be demoralizing and frustrating. Sorting through them to find an email you need to retrieve can be even worse. Careful application of each of the following strategies can reduce the amount of email you receive, ensure that the emails you send are more effective (and that replies you receive will likewise be more effective), and decrease the amount of time you must spend handling email.

Your supreme goal should be to reach "In-Box Empty," when you have no emails remaining in your in-box after you complete your periodic email processing. Because many lawyers start at "In-Box: Several Hundred" (or Several Thousand), this chapter will first walk you through how to manage the email that is coming in today, and it will conclude with some quick steps to get you to In-Box Empty in a short time. If you are facing a crowded in-box and feeling overwhelmed or discouraged, you might skip to page 106 to learn how to reach In-Box Empty almost immediately—but *heed this warning*: unless you read and apply the email strategies shared here, reaching In-Box Empty will be an ephemeral and ultimately useless exercise.

Handling the Email You Receive

Check your email only at predefined intervals, absolutely no more than once an hour. Even better, decrease the frequency and check email only twice daily, ideally in the midmorning and midafternoon. Do not check email first thing in the morning except to scan for emergencies. It is far too easy to get sucked into reading and responding to email, handling "just one more thing" over and over until an hour or more has vanished in a whirlwind of necessary but untrackable activity. When you are responding rapid-fire to a stack of email addressing a variety of client matters, it is difficult to bill for that time. Even more importantly, you may lose the high-energy morning hours to routine email processing rather than using that time to get your top priority items accomplished.

When will you check your email? Identify the frequency and make a commitment here to stick to that schedule for at least two weeks, even if it feels uncomfortable. After two weeks, evaluate the effects and decide whether to continue with that schedule, modify it, or to return to your old habit.

_____

_____

If you have an assistant, allow him to access your emails and help him to understand what is and is not an emergency. Ask your assistant to check your email first thing in the morning and to monitor incoming email on an hourly basis so that he will catch emergencies quickly and alert you. If you do not have an assistant who can perform this gatekeeping task for you, and if you receive emergency emails, get in the habit of scanning your in-box to look for emergencies but not reading or responding to non-urgent email, no matter how tempting it might be to do so. Alternatively, explore whether you can create an automatic reply that notifies that who send you email that you check email only in the midmorning and midafternoon and requesting a telephone call if a matter demands a faster response. (If you are checking email more frequently than 2–3 times a day, using such a message is not necessary.)

Disable the audio or visual notification that you have received a new email. Like a ringing telephone, an email notification feels urgent. In truth, 99% of the time the message is not urgent. (Ninety percent of those 294 billion emails sent daily are spam and viruses, and most people find that the bulk of the email they receive is informational rather than requesting action.) Unlike a ringing telephone, an email notification is never urgent, because it merely advises you of a message that has been received, which you can read at that moment or hours later. You will never miss an email in the same way you might miss a telephone call. If you consider the research shared on page 61 about interruptions and the delays most people experience in returning to the task at hand, it will be immediately obvious why disabling an email notification will save you time.

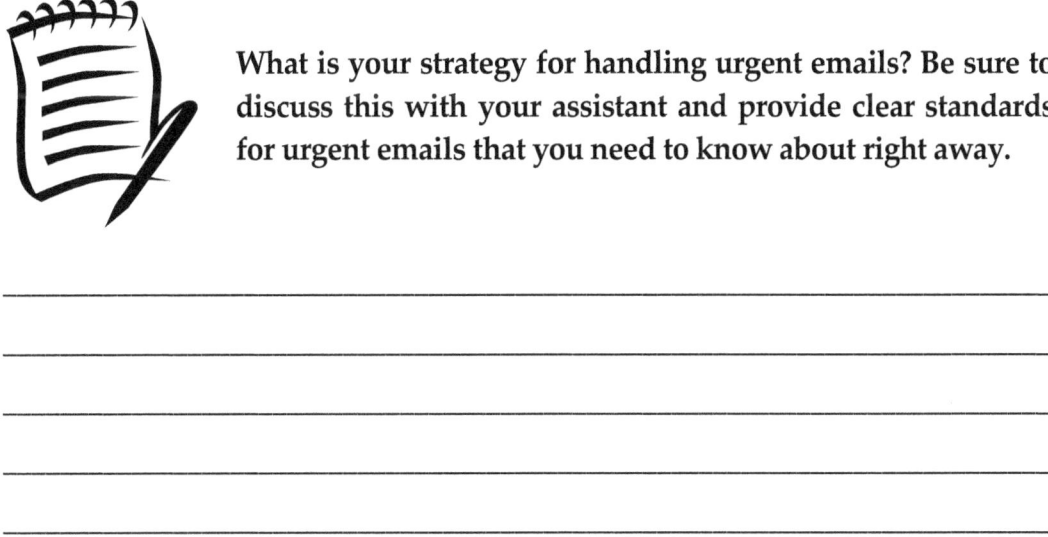

What is your strategy for handling urgent emails? Be sure to discuss this with your assistant and provide clear standards for urgent emails that you need to know about right away.

_____
_____
_____
_____

Use filters to reduce the amount of email in your in–box. Every email program has some sort of folder structure that allows you to sort and save

your emails according to any categories you create. Creating folders will allow you to use filters to send emails directly to the appropriate folder. For example, if you're an ABA member, unless you have opted out of the ABA email campaigns, you no doubt receive frequent emails about new ABA programs or products. You might create a folder titled ABA and create a filter that will scan the subject line or sender of incoming emails for "ABA," and to direct it to send those messages directly to the ABA folder. Describing how to set up filters is beyond the scope of *Seven Foundations*, given the number of email programs in use. Most programs have a Help function that will show you how to create folders, and almost any assistant (virtual or otherwise) can teach you how to use the most common programs.

One caution pertaining to the use of filters: do *not* set up filters for client matters. The risk of overlooking an urgent client email by using filters is simply too high. Filters typically bypass the in-box and place all filtered messages directly in folders, so you must open each folder containing new messages to see the sender, subject line, and priority level of new messages. Although you should request that clients call you for time-sensitive matters rather than emailing, some clients will send email despite such a request. Accidentally failing to open one folder could hide a critical email for several hours, and so it is safer to allow all client emails to go to your in-box rather than being filtered to folders.

When it is time to read and respond to your email—a task that is distinct from simply checking it for urgencies—**batch your email review**, using a similar process to clearing your paper in-box.

1. *Scan your email for urgencies*. During this step, delete anything that you can tell *immediately* does not require attention, such as a reminder of an appointment of which you are well aware or spam. Do not read any email, though, even if you know you will delete a message as soon as you have read it. The only purpose for this step is to find urgent emails that may be buried in your in-box.

2. *Read each email*.

    a. Delete or file every email that does not require a response.

Seven Foundations of Time Mastery for Attorneys

    b. If you can respond to an email in two minutes or less, do so.

    c. If an email will require a more in–depth response:

        i. If you are checking email on an hourly basis, move the mail to a folder labeled "Respond Later," and return to it during your designated time to deal with correspondence.

        ii. If you are checking email only two or three times daily and processing your email fully during that time, respond to each email. Be sure to keep track of your time, if billable. Your initial review of your in–box will allow you to address all emails pertinent to a particular matter in one block, which will facilitate billing for your email review.

    d. *File or delete* each email after sending your response.

Using this process and the time blocking recommended in Foundation Five, you will usually be able to respond to every email within a few hours of receipt. However, you will undoubtedly be under unusual pressure on occasion, if (for example) you are preparing for a trial or a big deal, or engaged in negotiations. In these instances, you may need to defer responding to all but the most urgent emails for a few days or longer.

> **If you cannot respond quickly to a message, at least acknowledge the email.**

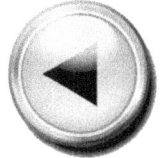

Unfortunately, many people have developed an unreasonable expectation that if you receive an email, you will read it within a very short time and you will respond within a few hours at most. **If you cannot respond quickly to a message, at least acknowledge the email.** Let the sender know that you received the email, and tell her when you expect to respond to it. You can even create a template that reads, "I've received your email. I'll be back in touch with you within *x amount of time*." When you send this message, you will reduce the likelihood that a sender will feel the

need to call and inquire whether you received her email. Taking the few seconds required to acknowledge the communication (or delegating that task to your assistant) will save you from an unnecessary interruption.

If you know you are going to be away from your office for more than a few hours, use an out–of–office autoresponder. An autoresponder is an automatic message that is sent as a response to each email you receive. The message informs the original sender that you are away from your office and eliminates their expectant waiting for your response so that it does not turn into frustration. You can draft the message to include information about whether and how often you will check email and/or voicemail, as well as contact information for someone who can handle any urgencies that arise in your absence. Using an out–of–office message will protect you from returning to the office to find numerous emails asking whether you received a previous email or voicemails that clog up your system.

Eliminate undesired email. Chances are that you receive two kinds of undesired email: spam and messages that you agreed to receive because you thought they'd be helpful, though you no longer wish to receive them. Eliminating each of these categories of email requires a different approach.

Spam is email that you receive without your permission. Pharmaceutical sales and "nominations" for graduate degrees are clearly spam, as is any unsolicited commercial email. Very often, unsubscribing from spam using an unsubscribe link will simply identify your email address as valid, and your address will likely be sold to other spammers. Instead of eliminating spam, you will likely end up with substantially more. Use a spam blocker instead.

Spam blockers operate in three different ways. The first uses a "white list," through which you create a list of people whose emails you do want to receive. Emails from the listed senders reach you directly, and those senders never even know you are using a spam blocker. Other senders who are not on your white list will have an opportunity to authenticate themselves or to request to be approved by you. Following authentication, that person is added to your white list, and you will receive their emails in the future without the need for further verification.

The second type of spam blocker quarantines suspected spam and sends it to a folder that you can review to retrieve any legitimate emails that end up in the folder by mistake. If you use this kind of spam blocker, be sure to check your spam folder each time you process your mail. If you check the spam folder frequently, skimming for legitimate mail will be easy; if not, doing so will become a massive chore.

The third type of spam blocker creates a "server–side" block to spam: it prevents some or all email that it believes to be spam from reaching your in–box. If you use this kind of spam blocker, do so with care since you may discover that you and the spam blocker have divergent ideas of what constitutes spam. If your firm uses a server–side spam blocker, be sure that you have some way to determine what emails are being blocked or some way to ensure that your client's emails arrive in your in–box.

Legitimate but unwanted email ("bacn") is distinct from spam. You may have subscribed (either voluntarily or by membership in a group) to newsletters from bar associations, those who provide services to lawyers, catalogs, and the like. Please note this distinction between spam and authorized but undesired email: those who send legitimate email will almost always respect your request to unsubscribe and will not sell your email address as spammers do. All responsible (and legally compliant) email subscription lists include an unsubscribe link somewhere above or at the bottom of the email, or you can respond to the message and request to be unsubscribed. Take a stringent approach to eliminating unwanted email: you can always resubscribe if you discover that you miss receiving the messages.

Finally, you will note than many email clients have a "Report Spam" option. Use that option only for emails that you did not request to receive. If you click on "Report Spam" in response to a mailing that you requested but no longer wish to receive, chances are good that you will continue to receive the mailing (because no "unsubscribe" request is transmitted to the sender) and that the person or organization sending the mail will be penalized for sending unsolicited mail.

 *Seven Foundations of Time Mastery for Attorneys*

Sending Email

The initial consideration in sending an email message is whether email is the best medium for your communication. Many lawyers are in the habit of shooting off an email as soon as we think of something, because as soon as the email is sent, we can mentally mark the topic as someone else's problem. In fact, a number of law firms have observed that younger associates may send an email to a partner to request that the partner address some aspect of a project assigned to the associate and that the associate considers a matter handled once she's emailed the partner. Thus, if a decision must be made, the partner is on the hook and the associate is out of the loop—at least in the eyes of the associate. That approach fails to benefit either associates' professional development or orderly workflow.

> **Ask yourself: Is email the best way to communicate this information to this person?**

Most of us tend to have a very short time between "I need to communicate this," and "I will send an email." The foundational question should be, **is email the best way to communicate this information to this person?** Problems arise with email communications all too frequently, and just because an email has been sent does not mean that the recipient will take note of it, act on it, or even receive it. The email may go astray or be delayed or some miscommunication could ensue—a common result when an email is drafted without due care. Possibly the communication could be handled more effectively by telephone or, for intra-office communications, by a quick in-person chat. If any of these challenges would create consequences of any magnitude, an email is not the best way to communicate.

Moreover, studies show that every email sent tends to generate at least two emails in response. The follow-up emails may be a conversation or a response from members of a group to whom the email was directed. However they come, they will add to your in–box, and caution is in order if you are aiming to reach In–Box Empty.

Decide Whether to Send an Email

Questioning whether it is necessary to send an email is one of the quickest ways to rein in the number of emails you receive and to eliminate the headaches your emails may generate. Here are some circumstances in which email is *not* the most effective form of communication:

1. **Do not send an email when a topic requires back–and–forth negotiation,** for example, if a group of six is trying to identify a date and time for a meeting. In other instances, you might not anticipate the need for several rounds of negotiation—if only two people are trying to find a time to meet, for instance. If you have sent an email and three replies have been generated without reaching a conclusion, pick up the telephone. Do not send that fourth email.

2. **Do not send an email for a request with a short deadline.** Your recipient may be out of the office or otherwise occupied, or he may have decided to check email only twice a day. As previously discussed, he should have an automatic message prepared to let you know his status, but many people skip this simple step. If you need an answer in four hours and spend three hours waiting for a response to an email, you will likely create an unnecessary crisis. Call instead.

3. **Do not send an email if your topic is complicated, if you need to address a lot of issues, of if you must resolve a series of dependent questions**. Especially with so many people checking emails on PDAs (Blackberries, iPhones, and the like), sending long and involved emails may be dangerous. For example, suppose you send an email that asks, "Is March 13th a good date for the meeting with opposing

counsel to discuss our discovery objections? Should we present the privilege argument, and do you think that I should attend?" If you receive a response that says only, "Yes," what question was answered? Page 102 of *Seven Foundations* will suggest some techniques for making an email clear even if it addresses multiple issues. If a complicated topic requires discussion, however, email probably is not the best medium to begin that conversation. Instead, arrange a time to talk in person or by telephone.

4. **Do not send an email to convey bad news.** This standard requires your discretion, because bad news may range from inconvenient to catastrophic. To decide whether an email is the appropriate way to deliver bad news, think about the recipient and how she will receive this news. If she is likely to be devastated, if she will need to ask questions to understand the impact of the news, you would be better advised to place a telephone call or to meet in person. Consider too what should occur after you convey the news: if you will need to discuss next steps immediately, email would not be the best mode of communication.

5. **Do not send an email if the recipient must hear your tone to receive the message you intend to convey.** Too often, we may write an email rather colloquially, with humor, sarcasm, or ironic understatement. Sending a message that can be read in more than one way creates the risk of miscommunication and even offending the recipient. Do not send tongue–in–cheek emails unless there is no possibility of misunderstanding your tone—and be aware that a good chance of miscommunication always exists for anything other than strictly factual statements.

As the foregoing list implies, emails work best when they are simple, when they do not require an immediate response, when they are limited to a few issues, when they are unlikely to provoke confusion or distress in the recipient, and when they are straightforward. Make it a habit to ask yourself, "Is this message best conveyed by email?" *before* you hit send.

Address Email and Name Recipients

When you address your emails, think about why you are including each recipient, and consider the implications of naming addressees as "To" recipients as compared with "cc" or "bcc" recipients. When you do send a "cc" or a "bcc," let the recipient know why he was included on the email. The reason may be apparent on the face of the message, or you may have a general operating procedure with a supervising attorney (in which case a "cc" may be designed to keep her informed about what is happening in the relevant client matter) or with your assistant (in which case a "bcc" may be her indication to docket dates or to prepare a letter to confirm an agreement). Whatever your operating procedure is, establishing it explicitly will save a lot of time–consuming questions and avoid miscommunication.

> When you address your emails, think about why you are including each recipient, and consider the implications of naming addressees as "To" recipients as compared with "cc" or "bcc" recipients.

Beware of the email address auto–fill feature. Many email programs include an auto–fill function that allows you to type the first few letters of a name, and then the program automatically supplies the first matching name. For instance, if you type "John," the program will automatically complete the address line with the first John in your contacts folder. Danger arises, of course, when you mean to send the message to John Zander and you have a John Ashe in your contacts. If you fail to notice the error, your email will be delivered to John Ashe, which could be problematic. In early 2008, a news story hit the general media when a litigator who was trying to discuss settlement of a massive case with a colleague accidentally sent the email to a reporter because of an auto–fill error. This kind of error is always embarrassing and can compromise a client's interest all too easily. Beware.

Seven Foundations of Time Mastery for Attorneys

Use a Descriptive Subject Line

Nonspecific email subject lines (like "hi" or "consultation" or "help"—or, worse yet, nothing at all) create unnecessary headaches. It is almost impossible to evaluate whether the email is urgent or important, and recipients may find it difficult to retrieve the email later to recapture whatever information might have been included because the subject line gives no hint of the actual subject matter. **Make your email subject lines specific and clear**, using the following techniques.

1. **Consider using subject line "flags."** These flags let the recipient know immediately why she's receiving the message, what action she needs to take and when. Examples of subject line flags include:

    a. FYI—For your information (implies no action necessary).

    b. NRN—No response necessary (implies FYI).

    c. RR—Response required, most useful when a date is included.

    d. AR—Action required, most useful when a date is included.

    e. EOM—End of message. Follows a subject line that conveys the entire message. For example, "Team meeting today, 3 PM, conference room A. EOM"

    Be sure that the recipients of your emails know what the flags mean. You will not save any time or avoid clogging your in-box if you send an email with "NRN" in the subject line and receive multiple responses asking what NRN means.

> Make your email subject lines specific and clear. The cardinal question is how to make the subject line convey as much as possible about what is in the email so that the topic is readily identifiable right away and easily searched for future retrieval.

 What email flags might be appropriate for the messages you send? Watch for anything that you repeatedly write in emails, and create a shorthand code. Ask your assistant and/or colleagues whether they can identify any useful flags. Be creative, but most importantly, keep your eye on what will be useful.

___

2. **Use a subject line that reflects what is in the email.** Your goal is to create a subject line that identifies the topic of the message sufficiently to alert the recipient and to make the message easy to find should you need to retrieve it in the future.

For example, suppose you bump into a colleague at the coffee machine one afternoon, and she says, "Hey, do you remember the date when the Williams trust instrument was executed?" You answer, "No, I don't know off the top of my head. Let me look it up. I'll get back to you. I'll shoot you an email."

As an aside, this situation is ideally suited to email. The content will be clear and simple (assuming no unusual circumstances), and your recipient will know precisely why she is receiving the information and what to do with it. Even if your colleague needs the information urgently, you have let her know to watch for an email from you, and if she tells you she needs it right away, you would call in addition or instead. When you pause to consider whether this is a message well-suited to email, your immediate answer will be affirmative. Now, how do you title that email? Consider these possibilities:

Seven Foundations of Time Mastery for Attorneys

    a. *"Trust Instrument Execution."* If the email arrives right away, your recipient will probably remember the conversation and know what information will likely be included. If one of you needs to search email archives later to find the same information, however, retrieving this email will be challenging. The subject line does not include the name of the trust at issue, so you will not necessarily recognize the email when you read the subject line. This is not a bad subject line (in comparison to, for instance, "answer"), but it is not particularly helpful.

    b. *"Williams Trust Instrument."* Because the subject line specifically identifies which trust is discussed in the email, this is a better subject line than the previous. It tells you generally what this email addresses. It does not identify the topic specifically, though, since the message could include any aspect of information about the Williams trust instrument.

    c. *"Williams Trust Instrument Execution Date."* Better still. This subject line identifies specifically what information is included. If you are searching for it even years later, when you see this subject, you will have a reasonably good sense of what is in the email, because it is clear that the message concerns the date of execution of the Williams trust instrument.

    d. *"NRN Williams Trust Instrument Execution Date 2/21/06. EOM."* Assuming that you have discussed the use of flags with your colleague and that NRN and EOM will not look like alphabet soup to her, this is an ideal subject line. It is precise, clear, and brief. All of the necessary information is in the subject line, and you have made it clear that no response is necessary. Your colleague can simply look at the subject line, and she has the answer—and the email exchange is done.

3. **Change the subject line as necessary.** If an email generates a series of responses and replies, the topic of conversation will often change over the course of the email chain. Make sure you change the subject

line to reflect the true subject of the email, both to assist the recipients (as well as yourself) in recognizing the topic of the email at a glance and to facilitate later retrieval.

For example, if the opening email addresses the viability of an argument that you want to make in a brief, the subject line might be, "Smith v. Jones, potential argument for MSJ?" Suppose that you and the email recipients exchange a few messages on that topic and then shift to a discussion of what testimony you would need to pull from Smith's deposition to support the arguments you plan to put forth. Because the topic of the email has shifted from a focus on whether to make the argument at all to how to support all of the anticipated arguments, you should change the subject line. A better subject line at that point might be, "Evidence from Smith Deposition to support MSJ." As always, the cardinal question is how to make the subject line convey as much as possible about what is in the email so that the topic is readily identifiable right away and easily searched for future retrieval.

Limit the Content of the Email

Do not send emails that deal with more than one subject. In other words, do not combine discussions about the Smith matter and the Jones matter into one email, unless the content is identical, such as reporting that opposing counsel has filed a leave of absence in both cases. The reason for this is simple: if you combine two subjects into a single email and write a subject line that adequately identifies both subjects, the subject line will be unwieldy and quite likely confusing. Moreover, you run the risk of catching your reader's attention on only one of the subjects—a risk that increases dramatically if your recipient reads the email on a PDA rather than on a full-sized screen, where both subjects are more likely to be visually noticeable.

Include no more than three issues within a subject, up to five at an absolute maximum. For instance, if you are addressing your concerns about the patentability of a new compound in view of a reference you found on

Medline, that reflects a single subject (patentability of the compound) and a single issue (potential anticipation by the Medline reference). If you include other references that disclose the compound, it is still a single issue. However, if you add in your concerns about inventorship as listed in the application, about potential complications because of the involvement of joint venture partners, and worries that scientists will disclose too much information about the compound at an upcoming conference, the email will swell to four issues, and it will start to become unmanageable.

To decide when an email has hit its limit of issues, imagine the subject line: "Potential anticipation of Compound *OPQ*" vs. "Compound *OPQ*: Potential anticipation, inventorship issues, JV complications, and potential disclosure at conference 12/14/08." If the subject line is long and unclear, the email is attempting to address too many issues.

If you must have multiple issues within an email, number them so that readers can follow along. Using the example above, the body of your email might look something like this:

1. **Anticipation**: I am concerned that Compound *OPQ* may be anticipated by several recently–discovered references, and thus unpatentable.

    a. Medline article [discuss]

    b. Catalog reference [discuss]

    c. Paper from 2006 Chemical Congress [discuss]

2. **Inventorship**: The named inventors on the draft application for Compound *OPQ* may be incorrect. [discuss]

3. **Potential disclosure at conference 12/14/08**: Several of the inventors are due to speak at the conference, and we must review their presentations to be sure that they do not disclose Compound *OPQ*, or we must file the application by 12/13/08.

    (Those knowledgeable about patents will appreciate that the subject line for such an email might be *Compound OPQ: concerns about patentability*. The subject line describes the general topic, which each

Seven Foundations of Time Mastery for Attorneys

numbered issue then explains. However, because patentability is a general term that encompasses many subtopics, "concerns about patentability" is not an ideal subject line.)

Including an outline format in emails that address multiple topics makes it easier for your readers to follow. The outline format creates visual markers of the various issues, which decreases the risk that a reader will overlook a key question or point. In addition, responses are simpler to write and to understand, because most lawyers will use the outline format provided and will structure their response accordingly. Instead of receiving an answer that includes several paragraphs that run together, you are likely to get an outline–form response.

Ask Questions Clearly

When you include questions or requests in an email, make them clear, easy to recognize, and simple to answer. For example, as previously discussed, it is a mistake to send a message that includes a series of questions such as, "Is March 13th a good date for the meeting with opposing counsel to discuss our discovery objections? Should we present the privilege argument, and do you think that I should attend?" Especially if he is reading quickly or reviewing email on a PDA, the recipient may see only two question marks and answer two questions instead of the three you posed. Or he may send an abbreviated response like, "Yes, no, no," which appears to be clear since you would likely assume that the order of the answers matches the order of the questions, but being wrong in that assumption could pose a significant problem.

> When you include questions or requests in an email, make them clear, easy to recognize, and simple to answer.

Make your requests cleanly. If you are asking three questions, number them. To continue our example, you might send an email that reads, "1. Is March 17th convenient? 2. Should we suggest this argument? 3. Should I attend?" Ideally you will receive a response that says "1. Yes. 2. No. 3. Yes," or something similar. You may not get a response that is quite that clear, but separating the questions increases the likelihood that you will not receive a one-word answer.

Reply to Email

Consider whether a reply to an email is necessary, or whether it is merely noise. Each email you send tends to generate two emails in response. If you reply to every email you receive, you are likely to increase the volume of your in-box dramatically. Especially with your assistant and colleagues, say "thank you" once, but do not make a habit of saying thanks every time someone gives you information by email. Though the intent is good, repeated thanks add to the tsunami of emails. Sometimes (especially when discussed in advance) silence is the best thanks you can give.

When you do send a reply, notice who was copied on the original email and consider whether each person should be copied on the reply. As previously discussed, unless a reason exists to copy recipients on an email, deleting them may reduce email traffic without impairing the transmission of information.

Finally, beware the "Reply to All" button when responding to an email message. Almost everyone has heard a terrifying story about a lawyer who accidentally sent information to opposing counsel or rude comments to an entire law firm. Always, *always* check the names listed on each email before you hit "send."

> Be sure your folders match your paper files so that you know where to start looking when you do need to look for an email.

Retaining Email Messages

Retaining emails electronically generally calls for one of two approaches: the "file" and the "dump." The previous discussion of using filters touched on **the "file" approach**, in which you create multiple electronic folders to reflect the categories of email you receive. Ease of filing and retrieval suggests creating a series of email folders that mirror your paper files. For instance, you will have a parent folder saved for each client with subfolders for each matter, and sub-subfolders as necessary. You might also create administrative folders for firm- or practice-related messages, bar association folders, and the like. Be sure your folders match your paper files (a great task to delegate) so that you know where to start looking when you need to look for an email. Of course, as with paper files, you do need to be careful to keep your folders in a sensible order so that when you get an email you know which folder it will go into and so that you know which folder is most likely to contain a particular email when you search for it.

The "dump" approach calls for a single electronic folder into which you place all of your saved emails. Every single email that you want to save goes in that folder regardless of the topic or the date. When you want to find a particular email, you do a text search that will highlight the result. Although some lawyers use the "dump" method with great success, search limitations may make it ineffective to use this system. Searching through one or a few email folders that cover the subject of the email for which you are searching tends to be fairly quick, and the visual cues are better organized because every email in a given folder will be on the same topic. If you only have one saved email folder, searching can be more complicated and can take longer, and scanning for an email is less likely to succeed because you will be scanning a mélange of client, administrative, news, and possibly even personal messages.

A third approach exists as well: **print key emails and maintain them in paper files.** However, doing so undermines the advantage of electronic storage that does not require physical space, and it also removes the aid of computer-powered searching. Print emails only if you plan to do something

with them (perhaps to use an email as a checklist) in which case you may find it simple to print the message, use it, and then throw it away. Some lawyers like to keep a notebook of correspondence; if you find this helpful, be sure to keep only the latest in a string of emails as long as all prior emails in the string are included. So, for example, if you send an email, print it out and put it in a notebook. When you receive a response that includes the text of your initial email, remove your original email from the notebook and substitute the later email. Otherwise, you can easily amass an enormous notebook filled with repetitions of the same email.

Dealing with Email Attachments

Managing email messages with attachments requires special mention because you are not only dealing with the email itself but also the attachment, which often must be printed. Use the email retention approaches previously discussed as well as the paper document retention techniques, and consider whether you need to retain the email attachment electronically as well.

No mention of email attachments would be complete without a warning to be careful when opening an attachment. Spam blockers generally include some kind of virus protection, but you are the first line of defense against any email that reaches your in-box. If you receive an email with an attachment from someone you do not know, or even if the email appears to be from a known source but something seems "off" about it (a typo-laden email from a meticulous typist, for example), be wary.

Reaching In-Box Empty

Contrary to what many people seem to believe, an email in-box is not a storage file, and it is not designed to maintain messages until you eventually have a chance to handle them. It is not a tickler file. An email in-box is simply a place for unread emails to live until they are handled, and that

Seven Foundations of Time Mastery for Attorneys

handling should occur relatively soon after the email has been received. The goal is to process your in–box until no emails remain. This is *In–Box Empty*.

> An email in–box is not a storage file, and it is not designed to maintain messages until you eventually have a chance to handle them.

If you have been using your in–box for storage, it may not be realistic for you to stop everything right now and process your in–box to zero. And yet, seeing an in–box with several hundred or, worse yet, several thousand emails can be demoralizing. So, consider the following two routes that will take you to In–Box Empty immediately.

The more radical of these two is **email bankruptcy**. Lawrence Lessig, a Stanford University professor of law, coined this term in 2004. After he had spent 80 hours attempting to clear out his email in–box, he declared bankruptcy by using the following steps:

1. *Create a list of the email addresses of everyone to whom you owe a response.*

2. *Create a mass email bcc'ing all of those addressees and explain your dilemma.* Craft an apologetic and sincere message that explains that you have fallen hopelessly behind on email, that you are declaring bankruptcy to get a fresh start, and that you will keep up with your messages in the future. (Be absolutely certain the recipients are bcc'ed, since sharing email addresses in a mass email is rude email etiquette and almost guarantees angry responses.)

3. *Ask recipients to resend any pressing messages.* Make sure you give priority attention to those messages as a matter of courtesy.

You should not ever send an "email bankruptcy" message to clients or opposing counsel, of course. Indeed, you should consider carefully which of

your professional contacts you would include on the email. If you feel there is no other option, email bankruptcy can be a good solution to a thorny problem.

Fortunately, however, a less drastic (and public) option does exist. Create an electronic folder labeled **Dump [Date]** and move your in–box into that folder. You have created In–Box Empty immediately—though, of course, you must still plow through your dump folder. Block out two or three two-hour periods and process the folder bit by bit during that time, using these tips, always remembering to watch for urgent messages:

1. **Sort the folder by sender.** Sorting by sender will let you drill down quickly based on how important the information is likely to be from a particular email correspondent. Use the email management strategies provided on page 90.

    a. If you find **emails from clients, opposing counsel, or other professional contacts** that require attention, handle those emails first. Be sure you have a method to highlight or flag those emails, or move them to a folder labeled "Respond ASAP" or similar. Whatever you do, do not allow them to recede back into the chaos. These are your most important emails.

    b. Delete any **emails from retailers and spammers**. Yes, you might miss the deal of the century, but it is unlikely—and certainly not your top concern.

    c. You will probably find many **emails that contain good information**—perhaps ABA newsletters or other newsletters that you find useful (maybe even my newsletter *Ignite!*). If you have so many emails that you feel the need to dump your in-box and start fresh, you will not be able to absorb those resources. Delete them.

2. **Sort the folder by subject.** Sorting by subject may help you recognize those emails that are not important.

    a. Delete or file everything that does not require a response. (And note that the standard is "require," not call for or deserve. Your goal is to streamline.)

b. If you can respond to an email within two minutes, do so.

c. If the response will take more than two minutes, highlight or flag the email or move it to a follow-up folder.

3. **Respond to all of the emails you have marked for follow-up.** This step will require the bulk of your time. Set a goal to have it completed in no more than a week.

4. **Resolve to maintain In-Box Empty going forward.** You will find that your in-box may swell during particularly busy periods, when you are traveling, or when you are out of the office. However, as you get accustomed to hyper-speed processing with these steps, returning to In-Box Empty won't be as daunting a prospect as it may be today.

If your in-box currently contains more than 50 emails, block out a time on your calendar to use one of these approaches to get to In-Box Empty immediately.

When will you commit to reaching In-Box Empty? (Be specific: date and time.) _____

Which approach will you use? _____

Working with PDAs

Working with PDAs (such as the BlackBerry®, iPhone®, etc.) brings advantages and disadvantages. When you can access your email from any location with a cell signal, you can truly disconnect from the office only if you do so intentionally. The email I received from Barbara (whom you met in Foundation One) read, "I think I need some help. I'm having trouble with time management and organization. It's 4:27 AM and I'm sitting in my bathroom, checking email here so I won't disturb my husband's sleep. I've been here since 3:30, when I woke up in a panic. I am exhausted and I am overwhelmed. I need help with managing my time. I can't keep doing this." That's extreme. Unfortunately, violation of work/life separation is not unusual when a PDA comes into play.

Most PDAs include an automatic script that places a signature "Sent from my BlackBerry®" or "Sent from my iPhone®" at the bottom of each email. Consider deleting that script so that it is less clear when you are out of the office. Once clients and colleagues know that you are accessible by email even when you are out of the office, you have lost some measure, possibly a significant measure, of control over your time.

You must also ensure that your PDA synchronizes with your primary computer in a way that works well for you. Some people want all emails to remain unread on the primary computer even if you read them via PDA, others want to have emails read on the PDA marked read in their primary email in-box. Whatever your preference, just be sure you can tell at a glance what you have and what you have not handled. Otherwise, your PDA usage may increase, not decrease, the time you must spend in dealing with your email.

> **Once clients and colleagues know that you are accessible by email even when you are out of the office, you have lost some measure of control over your time.**

Advantages of the PDA include the ability to get email anywhere. PDAs will now open most attachments so that you can read documents, and accordingly you are no longer restricted to working only in your office. PDAs can also sync with your online system for your calendar and your tasks as well as your email. That can be very helpful so that you know what appointments and tasks are on your list wherever you are.

Seven Foundations of Time Mastery for Attorneys

Whether a PDA makes your professional and personal life flow more easily or whether it disrupts both largely comes down to knowing how to discipline yourself to check your PDA at appropriate times, to put it on silent at appropriate times, and to turn it off at appropriate times. You must also commit to learning how to use it to its full capacity.

Final tips: Be sure that you synchronize your PDA with your primary email in-box so that you do not misplace emails between the two. Build a specified time for synchronization into your regular schedule so you do not forget this crucial step. Finally, when you send emails from a PDA, consider whether you will need a copy of the email you are sending. If emails sent from your PDA are not archived in your primary email account, you may need to send a copy to yourself.

> **Whether a PDA makes your professional and personal life flow more easily or whether it disrupts both largely comes down to knowing how to discipline yourself to check your PDA at appropriate times, to put it on silent at appropriate times, and to turn it off at appropriate times.**

Email Caveats

Consider the potential ethical implications of sending email. Take every possible step to avoid the inadvertent disclosure of information, and be aware of where your email could go. If you are about to email highly sensitive information, stop and think. If the information could cause trouble if it were to fall into the wrong hands or to end up on the front page of the newspaper, maybe you should not send it by email. There are no hard-and-fast rules on this, but stop to consider whether email is appropriate so that you will have the opportunity to exercise your judgment.

Do not allow yourself to be the person who makes the deadly, inadvertent disclosure. I once received an email from a lawyer with whom I had worked on bar association projects. The email appeared to be intended for a client or colleague, and it appeared to go into some detail about a pending matter. Since I am not his client or on his team, clearly the email was not intended for me. I responded and told him that I had received the email in error and deleted it without reading it. He replied, thanked me, and told me that he had intended to send the email to a Julie on his team, which explained how it the email was misdirected to me. About 15 minutes later I got another email from him. It was exactly the same email. It was addressed to me again as well as to another Julie.

Email can be dangerous. The more careful you are the less the danger, but danger cannot be removed entirely.

Email and Personal Connections

Email is easy—sometimes, too easy. Aside from the problems outlined above, overuse of email can retard the growth of personal connections. While using email can save a great deal of time (when used properly), be certain that you consider whether conversation that can advance a strategy or a relationship might outweigh saving some time by using email. You will also find that picking up the telephone or popping down the hall for a face-to-face conversation may yield better results than an email would.

The bottom line: always ask whether email is the best form of communication to meet your particular objectives. If so, use email carefully and for maximum effect. If not, let go of the temptation to take the easy way out.

Chapter Nine

Foundation 6: Work the Telephone

While telephone calls and voicemail messages are (like email) nonphysical, they are a part of the information tsunami. Clear and careful guidelines are required for effective management of telephone calls and voicemail.

Managing Telephone Calls

Set telephone appointments. Just as it is easy to have an idea and send an email, it is equally easy to pick up the telephone and call someone. However, you face slim odds that the person with whom you wish to speak will be available and ready to discuss whatever it is that you want to discuss at that moment. Instead, you (or your assistant) might schedule a telephone appointment, either by telephone or by email. To make telephone calls more effective, set an agenda, even if the agenda is only a short email agreeing on the topics you will discuss. None of these preliminary communications needs to be formal. A message can be both simple and effective, such as, "Let's get together by telephone at 3 on Friday afternoon. I will call you, and I'd like to discuss my objections to your written discovery."

Block out a time to return telephone calls. By dedicating a certain period

Seven Foundations of Time Mastery for Attorneys

of time when you will return non-urgent telephone calls, you will be able to manage your clients', opposing counsels' and other callers' expectations. You might even consider adding a statement to your outgoing voicemail message that lets callers know when you will return non-urgent calls. By batching your return calls, you will be able to get through them more quickly and (assuming you communicate your dedicated return call time slot) you will increase the chance of making contact when you do return the call.

> **Create a standard response for clients who need general information about an upcoming hearing or other matter that does not require your direct attention.**

Designate a member of your support staff to be responsible for responding to client contacts. Depending on your practice area, you might be able to create a standard response for clients who need general information about an upcoming hearing or other matter that does not require your direct attention. You might instruct a responsible staff member to let clients know when in the day you typically return telephone calls and to be sure that time will be convenient for the caller. The focus is to make sure that any urgent calls get handled immediately, so you will want to discuss what kinds of questions are urgent and to select an assistant with excellent judgment and people skills to be the first line of response for clients.

Keep a notepad by your telephone. Having a designated pad for telephone notes (preferably a spiral-bound pad so you stand less chance of losing the pages) ensures that any notes you take while on the telephone will be corralled in a single location for transcribing or for future reference. Be sure to note the time and date every time you write on the pad. This practice also creates a "memory jogger" for you, since you will be able to look back to a date and know quickly whether you had a substantive conversation with someone and, so, what you discussed.

Seven Foundations of Time Mastery for Attorneys

Voicemail

Create a useful outgoing message for your voicemail. A useful voicemail greeting includes the following information:

- Your name and law firm/corporation/government office name.

- Information early in the message about how to skip the rest of it, such as "please press the pound sign to go directly to voicemail without hearing the rest of this message."

- Directions telling callers how to reach a human being and during what hours she may do so. For example, "Please press zero to reach an operator between 8 A.M. and 6 P.M."

- If you have an assistant, include information about how to reach him. ("If you have an urgent question, please contact Pat at [a phone number]."

- If you are out of the office, say so. This courtesy prevents a caller's frustration that arises from leaving an urgent voicemail with no idea that you're out of the office.

 If your current outgoing voicemail message does not include all of these components, it is time for a change. Draft your new voicemail greeting here. As soon as you finish writing it, record it.

_____

_____

_____

_____

_____

If you are out of the office for a long absence, record a temporary voicemail greeting with that information. I worked with someone a few years ago ("Susan") who traveled to Bali for vacation. She would be completely inaccessible while she was there—no voicemail or email. Susan had informed all of her colleagues and the support staff with whom she worked when and where she was going, not just once but multiple times. She even gave a written memo to her assistant and the law firm receptionist, including a chart so that both could easily see to whom questions about particular matters should be referred. Despite all of those preparations, Susan did not record a temporary voicemail greeting to let callers know that she was out of the office.

After she had been gone only a few days, a partner (who happened to be the partner in charge of her practice group) needed something urgently. He had forgotten that Susan was out of the office. He needed to talk with her immediately and could not find her assistant, so he started leaving voicemails for Susan. When she returned to her office after her vacation, she found a multitude of increasingly angry voicemails. Her return from vacation was stressful and her reputation was damaged (fortunately, not permanently, since the partner remembered a few days after leaving the voicemails that Susan was away and that she had warned him repeatedly), and all of the angst and anger could easily have been avoided if only she had taken two minutes to record an "out of office" voicemail message.

When you leave a message or voicemail, make sure your message is clear. Be sure you:

- Include a slow rendition of your name and telephone number. Speak slowly and clearly.

- Explain, briefly, why you are calling. It is frustrating to receive a voicemail that says only, "John Smith. 555–1212. Please call me." If the person you are calling does not recognize your name or telephone number, he may be disinclined to return the call.

- Identify when the person you are calling is most likely reach you with a return telephone call. Just as you can batch your outgoing calls every day during preselected hours, you can set times when you will be available to receive phone calls. You will not always receive your calls in that time, of course, but if you say when you will be available others may try to reach you during those hours. The benefit of encouraging telephone calls during specific times is that you can be prepared for discussions that you anticipate, and you may be able to avoid having other work interrupted.

- Close your message, once again, with a slow repetition of your telephone number.

As with other commonly-used tools, a little extra attention to how you use the telephone is likely to pay significant dividends in enhancing your work flow.

Seven Foundations of Time Mastery for Attorneys

Chapter 10

Foundation 7: Set SMART goals

The purpose of the Seventh Foundation of Time Mastery is to create a structure that will assist you incorporating the first six Foundations in your life. Many of us prove annually that it is difficult to make a radical change in how we live. On January 1 each year, millions decide to live a "healthy life," and they resolve to give up sweets, to eat more fruits and vegetables, to exercise and lift weights every day, to meditate for 30 minutes every morning, or to quit drinking alcohol. (Some daring folks even resolve to undertake all of those goals at once!) Studies show that 25% of New Year's resolutions go by the wayside before the end of the first week, and only 46% of people keep their resolutions for six months or longer. How can you avoid the same fate for your time mastery plans? Set SMART goals.

> 25% of New Year's resolutions go by the wayside before the end of the first week, and only 46% of people keep their resolutions for six months or longer.

SMART is an acronym for Specific, Measurable, Achievable, Realistic, and Time–based. Poorly phrased goals leave you demoralized and feeling like a failure. A few examples:

- Setting *vague or unmeasurable goals* means that no matter how hard you work, you will not be able to say with certainty whether you reached your goals. If you say that you would like to improve your writing skills, for instance, you will be unable to claim success because there is no finish line—you could always improve your skills even more.

- Setting *unrealistic goals* guarantees failure. If you set a goal that no human could reach (such as reviewing 45,000 documents or drafting a complicated filing for the SEC in a single day), you will certainly finish the day without achieving your goal.

- Setting *goals unbounded by time* is setting a particular kind of vague goal, one in which you fail to define when you will check your progress. Accordingly, if you say that you would like to bill 200 hours, the goal is so unclear without a measurement of time that you could "succeed" by billing 2 hours a day for 100 days, even though you would almost certainly find yourself without a job or income as a result. Success? Not exactly.

How can you transform a poorly phrased goal into a SMART goal? A client ("Tom") once contacted me because he was unhappy in his work. He was uncertain whether he wanted to stay with the same firm, whether he wanted to move to another firm, whether he wanted to continue practicing in his current area of law, or whether he wanted to leave practice altogether. When I asked what he wanted to achieve from the coaching, Tom told me that his goal was to figure out how to design and lead the rest of his professional life. While that is not an unusual desire, it does not qualify as a SMART goal because it is vague and not time–based.

After our consultation, Tom hired me to coach him, and our first objective was to set a SMART goal for the engagement. Tom whittled his "what do I want to do with the rest of my life" down to a goal of deciding within two months whether to stay with his current firm. That's a SMART goal. It was specific: the answer he was seeking, yes or no, was very clear. The decision was specific to his current firm. It was measurable, because he

would conclude with a yes/no decision. It was achievable and realistic for Tom (he knew he was capable of reaching the decision within two months), and the goal was time–based.

Nearly any goal can be transformed into a SMART goal. "I want to be a better lawyer" is not specific, but "I want to be a better lawyer by communicating with my clients more effectively" is. But that is not a measurable goal (what does *more effective communication* mean?), so perhaps the goal would then become "I want to be a better lawyer by communicating more effectively with my clients: I will respond to all client inquiries within four business hours at least to acknowledge that the inquiry has been received." That's measurable. It is achievable, perhaps with the assistance of support staff members. Depending on the nature of this lawyer's practice, it may be realistic to have someone (staff or attorney) respond to each client inquiry within four business hours. And the goal is time–based, since the implication is that the effort will begin immediately. The final goal then would be worded, "Starting today, I will become a better lawyer by communicating more effectively with my clients as measured by having someone from my staff respond to every client inquiry within four hours." That shift is an example of transforming a good but rather nonspecific goal into a SMART goal.

Think of a goal you currently have. Is it a SMART goal? If not, reword it so that it is, and write the revised goal here.

_____

_____

_____

_____

According to a study performed by the American Society for Training and Development, the likelihood of a person completing a goal varies depending on how the person sets the goal, as follows:

- Hear an idea 10%
- Consciously decide to adopt an idea 25%
- Decide when you will do it 40%
- Plan how you will do it 50%
- Commit to someone else that you will do it 65%
- Have a specific accountability appointment with the person you committed to 95%

Consider what kind of support you will find helpful in achieving your goals.

If you have completed the exercises and actions suggested throughout this book, you have already made changes. You have already created at least some plans for how you will change your approach to time and to various practice–related tasks. What other support do you need to arrange to ensure that you will carry through on those plans?

How do you find support for achieving the goals you set, particularly in the area of time mastery? To whom will you commit to making the changes you've identified through the Seven Foundations? When will you meet with that person?

_____

_____

_____

_____

_____

Chapter Eleven

Conclusion

One of my favorite quotes that is applicable to lawyers and the practice of law is, "'Serenity is not freedom from the storm, but peace amid the storm." I have never located an attribution for that quote, but I like to think that a lawyer might have written it.

> **Productivity and efficiency depend on making sure that you are doing the right things at the right time.**

Productivity and efficiency depend on two things. The first is making sure that you are doing the right things, and second is doing them at the right time. The First Foundation (Manage Your Energy, Not Your Time) is fundamental to this two-step process because it ensures that you will be able to do the right things. The Second Foundation, Prioritize and Act Accordingly, ensures that you act at the right time, and the remaining foundations (Delegate Effectively, Manage Your Physical Environment, Tame the Email Tsunami, Work the Telephone, and Set SMART Goals) address the right things.

Seven Foundations of Time Mastery for Attorneys

If you have completed the exercises throughout this book, you have plans in place and may already have changed some of your behaviors. If you have not worked the exercises, return to the sections that seem most relevant to you and complete them now. Decide what you will do with this material now. All lawyers have had the experience of attending CLE or practice management seminars, receiving useful information that we fully intend to implement, and then returning to the office and getting sidetracked. Perhaps you have even purchased time management systems or books in the past and discovered that they are only "shelf help"—resources that sit on your bookshelf and accomplish nothing for you. Do not let that happen here. Take a few minutes to write down what are you going to implement.

 **What new habit will I begin to incorporate today? (Only one.)**

_____

_____

 **What new habits will I begin to incorporate this week? (A total of no more than three, including the new habit you've decided to begin incorporating today.)**

_____

_____

_____

_____

_____

Seven Foundations of Time Mastery for Attorneys

What new habits will I begin to incorporate this month? (A total of no more than five, including the habits you've decided to begin incorporating today and this week.)

_____
_____
_____
_____
_____

What new habits will I begin to incorporate this quarter? (A total of no more than seven, including the habits you've decided to begin incorporating today, this week, and this month.)

_____
_____
_____
_____
_____

How will I hold myself accountable for developing these new habits and practices?

Seven Foundations of Time Mastery for Attorneys

_____
_____
_____
_____
_____

What is possible when you learn to master your time? Michael hired me to work with him on transforming his practice. Tired of litigating small matters that kept him running every day, putting out fires and adding to his revenue in drips of two or three hundred dollars, Michael wanted to grow a related but substantially more sophisticated litigation practice that had presented itself as a new opportunity. Like most opportunities, though, this one came at a cost: to serve a new class of clients, Michael needed to completely revamp his practice. The changes included making the move from a being sole practitioner with only part–time administrative support to adding, in fairly quick succession, a paralegal, two associates, and two administrative assistants. Within eighteen months, Michael's practice was unrecognizable.

When we began working together, our focus was exclusively on business development and making the contacts necessary to exploit the new practice area. Michael soon began weaving concerns about time into our conversations, and he admitted that his marriage was in trouble because, he said, his workload kept him away from his home and his stress made him unpleasant when he was at home. He reluctantly acknowledged that divorce was inevitable unless something changed, and he agreed that he was neglecting some of the tasks necessary to grow his practice due to the additional stress that he felt because his marriage was dying. Michael loved his wife (at least, he thought he still did) and he did not want to disrupt his children's lives.

Even more alarmingly, Michael was experiencing chest pains and had received "the talk" from his doctor. He was in tears during one of our calls,

fearing that he would lose not only his marriage and family but also his life if he continued in the ruts he had carved. Given these concerns, it is perhaps no surprise that Michael had begun to miss deadlines. Although Michael's initial and primary focus had been building the new practice, his personal life soon provided the undercurrent that steered his practice development.

As all of Michael's circumstances became clear, I realized that time mastery would be a critical aspect of our work together. Starting with the First Foundation, Michael set aside twenty minutes for a daily walk. He soon discovered that the exercise made him feel better physically and also offered him much needed silence and time for reflection. Michael set aside time with each of his three children each week, and he found that he could be more focused on growing his practice when he wasn't as worried about his children and whether they felt that he neglected them in favor of his work. Michael and his wife began to talk again, and after reflection on a few of his walks, he realized that the reason he wanted to transform his practice was because he deeply missed his family and wanted to build a financially stable practice that would allow him to support his family and to spend time with them.

As we discussed how Michael would shift and grow his practice, he began to place priorities on meeting the kinds of business owners he wanted as clients. He continued to serve his "squeaky wheel" clients, and he decided that missing deadlines was no longer acceptable. Michael began to track that work he needed to do more closely, and he dedicated specific hours to clearing out the backlog of work that remained. As he completed each small matter, he turned away more of the same so that he would have the room in his practice to serve a different class of clients. Although he had a tricky balancing act at times between putting out fires for the "old practice" and recruiting the work to build his "new practice," Michael was able to focus on the practice he wanted to grow rather than only on the practice he had built to that point. The transition had its rocky moments, but by prioritizing the activities that would bring him the practice he wanted, Michael brought in more and more of the business he'd wanted for years but had never made the concerted effort to pursue.

Seven Foundations of Time Mastery for Attorneys

As his practice grew and he added new staff members to serve the new clients, Michael began to experiment with his leadership style. Always a micromanager, he hired staff members whose judgment he trusted and began to delegate entire projects to them. While the process of shifting from sole practitioner to senior partner was hardly a straight line, Michael worked to adjust his expectations and to hone his delegation skills. Communications with his staff and clients took a central role in Michael's days, and he adapted the Fifth Foundation email management strategies so that his email served his practice and did not engulf his working hours.

Through our work, Michael set and reached successive SMART goals. Over the course of our engagement, his practice shifted so that 75% of his time and revenue (which, despite the recession, was up substantially even after paying the new staff members) flowed from the new practice, and the remaining 25% of matters were closing out and being replaced. Michael and his wife had entered counseling and celebrated their anniversary with a second honeymoon. On his birthday, Michael's wife toasted him and told him that she felt that the changes he'd made had given her an improved version of the husband she'd been missing and the father their children had needed. And at his annual check–up, Michael's doctor congratulated him for losing weight and recapturing his health.

Michael's experience is extraordinary because he shifted not just his practice but also his personal satisfaction, his family life, and his health. The Seven Foundations underlay each of those shifts and were responsible for his success in maintaining the changes he made.

Think of Michael as your predecessor in walking the Seven Foundations path. Perhaps your objectives are not as radical as his, and your obstacles may not loom as large. Rest assured that if Michael was able to use the Seven Foundations to transform his life and practice, you will be able to reach your goals as well.

The economy and the business world in which we are now operating offers rewards for those who identify and work consistently toward their goals. Clients who are doing more with less have raised the bar for their attorneys, and success in practice now requires a higher level of performance than ever. You have spent years developing your substantive expertise. This is the time to develop a support structure to allow you to provide exceptional client service so that you can make the income and impact you want through your practice. Start today. You can make the changes you feel stirring. Your clients and your life are waiting. Go!

Additional Resources

Allen, David. *Getting Things Done: The Art of Stress–Free Productivity*. New York: Viking Penguin, 2001.

Covey, Stephen R. et al. *First Things First*. New York: Simon & Schuster, Inc., 1994.

Loehr, Jim and Swartz, Tony. *The Power of Full Engagement*. New York: Free Press, 2003.

Morgenstern, Julie. *Never Check E–Mail in the Morning*. New York: Simon & Schuster, Inc., 2004 (originally published as *Making Work Work*).

Schwartz, Tony; Gomes, Jean; McCarthy, Catherine. *The Way We're Working Isn't Working: The Four Forgotten Needs that Energize Great Performance*. New York: Free Press, 2010.

Productivity Goal
http://www.productivitygoal.com/

Life at the Bar Blog
http://www.lifeatthebar.com/blog

43 Folders
http://www.43folders.com

Note: 43 Folders has shifted from being a productivity blog to a blog "about finding the time and attention to do your best creative work." The blog is nonetheless an excellent resource for using and extending the techniques offered in *Getting Things Done*. In addition, the blog offers perhaps the best ever–so–slightly–off–color definition of productivity I've ever seen:

**"Productivity" isn't about making more widgets per hour
or being efficient and organized
for its own anal–retentive sake.
Real productivity means getting faster at
moving the crap off your desk
so you can have room to focus on
the creative work that only you can do.**

**Figure out how to do that every
morning, and you'll be ready to go pro.**

Appendix

Selected Time Management Posts from the Life at the Bar Blog

www.LifeAtTheBar.com/blog

Seven Foundations of Time Mastery for Attorneys

How to Build Habits and Routines that Enhance Your Reputation for Reliability: Masterful Timesheets and Client Communications

In addition to improving the effective use of your time, the Seven Foundations can also help you to establish habits and routines that will develop your reliability and your reputation for reliability.

Time Records

No lawyer enjoys keeping track of his time, but for many lawyers in private practice and for some lawyers who are in-house, it is a necessary evil—at least for now. (As you are no doubt aware, controversy has mounted about the benefits and drawbacks of the billable hour. However, keeping track of your time will always be a beneficial exercise, whether your time spent is related directly to your fees or you operate under flat fee or contingency plans.)

Timesheets also present a good opportunity to communicate with your clients about the work that you are performing on their behalf. You can use a computer system that, with a few clicks, will keep track of your time spent on a particular matter, or you can adapt a low-tech paper system. Whatever your approach to timesheets, keep your time as you work (no retrospective estimates, which often result in lost time) and ensure your description of your activities communicates clearly to your client what you did during the time recorded. Your clients will appreciate your avoiding vague language like "attention to file" in preference of detailed entries like, "reviewed and revised settlement agreement to incorporate additional terms concerning maintenance and disclosure of financial records." They will also pay their bills more quickly and dispute your fees less frequently.

> **Keep your time as you work (no retrospective estimates, which often result in lost time) and ensure your description of your activities communicates clearly to your client what you did during the time recorded.**

In addition, it is important to have a credible document in case a client audits your time or you receive an award of attorney's fees and need to be able to substantiate the propriety of your time. Credible documents are not those generated when you sit down on the last day of the month and try to reconstruct your time from a hodge-podge of memory, emails, documents, and assorted other records. That approach risks disaster and even discipline.

If you maintain your time on a consistent daily basis, and if you make it a habit of using your timesheets to "talk" to your clients about your activity on their behalf, you will enhance your credibility and professionalism. If not, embarrassment (or worse) may ensue.

Client Communications

More bar complaints are lodged against lawyers for failure to respond to client communications than for any other reason. Clients expect quick responses to their communications. Even if you know that a matter is routine and that nothing is afoot, most clients will consider their matter to be of pressing importance.

Generally, clients will be satisfied (at least for a time) as long as they receive *some* response to an inquiry, even if it is not a detailed or substantive response. From a lawyer's perspective, it is easy to look at an email (especially on the go on a PDA) or to listen to a voicemail, to absorb the message and then to put it out of mind if it does not call for a substantive response or action. You have moved on to the next concern, and you see no need to respond to the email or voicemail. Clients may overlook that once, but failing to respond to a client communication undermines your reputation for exceptional client service, and exceptional client service not only keeps your current clients satisfied but it earns you future business from those clients and from referrals

> **More bar complaints are lodged against lawyers for failure to respond to client communications than for any other reason.**

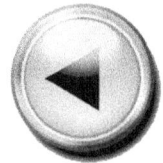

If you work with support staff, or with a virtual assistant, your staff can be tremendously helpful for you in fielding client communications. For instance, imagine that a client has sent an email or called your office to provide information that she wants you to have. Maybe you need it, maybe not, but she wants you to have it. You do not necessarily have to contact that client yourself to respond, though doing so (even via a personalized email template) will make a good impression. But you can create a system so that your staff will acknowledge every client communication within the time you dictate and, where necessary, will let the client know when he can expect to hear directly from you.

You can even take this a step further and design a system for proactive client contact. Have some sort of system that tracks the date of the last communication and contact the client either personally or through your staff. Let the client know the status of his matter or that all is quiet. If you educate your clients at the beginning of the representation what your practice is for communicating with clients, probably 90 percent of your clients will accept your structure.

Typically, trouble arises when clients do not know what to expect and they imagine the worst. You might tell a client, however, "My commitment to you is that someone from my office, myself or a staff person, will respond to every call you make to me, either within four hours or by 10 AM on the next business day if we receive your call after 2 PM." Of course, you can adapt this operating procedure to your practice and your preference. Having a system, educating your clients about it, and training your staff to implement it will create a reputation for reliability and responsiveness that will pay significant dividends.

PDA Peace: Eliminating Interruptions from PDAs

Pavlov's dog had nothing on most BlackBerry®/iPhone®/Android/other PDA users.

All too often, we hear the "beep" or feel the vibration and pounce immediately, even in the middle of a sentence—our own or someone else's. And I've seen (and though I'd prefer not to admit it, experienced) the discomfort that can occur when someone knows there's an email waiting but doesn't pounce. The ticks, the nervousness. It's almost pathological.

I once decided to drive for a business trip rather than fly. For safety's sake, I didn't want to be tempted to look at my BlackBerry® each time an email came in. So I set the profile to ring for phone calls only, and to be silent otherwise. I drove almost 150 miles before I had to stop for gas, and I checked the BlackBerry® then. I had about 40 messages, none of them urgent. And I had a strange feeling that I subsequently identified as peace. Peace! No irritating noises, no demands, no irrelevant press releases. It was a good change.

Since then, I've continued to keep my BlackBerry® on "phone only." If I'm expecting something urgent, I ask for a phone call rather than an email, and it's been instructive to discover how much better conversations are when I'm not wondering about the email I just heard arriving. And the truth is that I have yet to miss anything important as a result of this practice.

Try it. Just for today. You can change back tomorrow if you like. I predict you won't want to, and I predict you'll be more present to your work, the people you're with, even your own relaxation. And in turn, you'll be more productive and more creative.

Not a bad return on eliminating an irritant, is it?

 *Seven Foundations of Time Mastery for Attorneys*

Increasing Energy by Clearing Mental Clutter

Every office has one: the messy lawyer whose desk and/or office always looks like a bomb exploded, leaving behind papers and files and coffee cups and who–knows–what–else scattered everywhere. It's a good practice to clear the decks weekly or following the end of a major project, just to keep some level of tidiness. Especially if you can request an assistant to help with filing and organization, 30 minutes to an hour will often prevent an overflow.

What if it's your mind that needs decluttering? When your brain is filled with "must do" tasks of both professional and personal origin, when you're worried about something, when you're trying to make a difficult decision, and when all of your thoughts are further agitated by the "noise" of life, it's easy to get lost in mental chaos. One day when I was preparing for a major client meeting and dealing with my mother's terminal illness, I stopped by the grocery store on my way home. I knew I was distracted, so I'd taken the time to write down the items I needed to buy. But I proved how distracted I was when I returned to my car to find it still running with the keys in the ignition.

The Zen Habits blog recommends 15 Can't–Miss Ways to Declutter Your Mind. The tactics are as follows:

> Breathe
> Write it down
> Identify the essential

    Eliminate
    Journal
    Rethink your sleep
    Take a walk
    Watch less TV
    Get in touch with nature
    Do less
    Go slower
    Let go
    Declutter your surroundings
    Single–task
    Get a load off (Vent!)

(The full post is available at http://zenhabits.net/2007/12/15–cant–miss–ways–to–declutter–your–mind/.)

I'd add one more tactic: do something creative that gets you into a state of flow, where time passes without your notice. Examples might be drawing or playing music. Time spent in any of these areas is indeed time well spent, and reducing your mental clutter will increase your energy.

Recreation: A Foundation of Balance and Productivity

At least one activity exists that, perhaps counter–intuitively, is a foundation of both work/life balance and productivity: recreation.

While coaching a client and introducing Stephen Covey's Urgent/Important quadrant system for prioritizing and completing tasks, I explained that true recreation—something that's reenergizing, that "re–creates," rather than passive activities like vegging out in front of the TV—is a Quadrant II activity: not urgent, but important. It isn't urgent because there will never be a requirement to enjoy recreation. No one will ever request you to "recreate" on their time schedule, and no law firm partner will ever drop by late in the afternoon and apologize for asking you to put in a few hours of recreation that night. (Absurd image, isn't it?) But it's vitally important.

What "true recreation"? It varies from person to person. Perhaps it's writing, gardening, skiing, going to or performing in the theatre, playing with children, doing volunteer work… Whatever it is that takes a person from his ordinary self into a state of flow, where time passes without notice and the end result is production of energy, enthusiasm, a rounded person. The key point is that true recreation creates balance and energy, both of which lead to increased productivity in the office. And that's what makes it important.

For those of you who are inclined to try an experiment, give this a shot: if you typically eat lunch at your desk, try going out instead. Spend 30 or 45 minutes at a museum, in a park, talking with a friend, whatever you enjoy. And don't check voicemail or email or answer your cell phone while you're away from the office.

Notice whether you're more productive than usual when you get back to your desk in the afternoon. Or take several hours over the weekend to engage in recreation, and notice the effects when you get back to work. The energy you increase through true recreation will pay dividends in productivity.

Are You Busy—or Productive?

One of the most important tools of coaching rests in illuminating distinctions. I have several favorites that come up in the course of a great many coaching engagements: reaction vs. response, hearing vs. listening, assertion vs. assessment, interesting vs. purposeful, and so on. One distinction is particularly relevant to effective action: busy vs. productive.

My favorite definition of *busy* is "full of or characterized by activity." Another definition of busy (often used as in a pattern or design, but still relevant here) is "cluttered with detail to the point of being distracting." *Productive* is, of course, derived from the verb to produce, and my favorite definitions of to produce are "to create by physical or mental effort" and "to bring into existence; give rise to; cause."

We seem to live in a culture that embraces busyness and has made it a virtue to be busy. And yet, I'm taken by the idea that being busy can mean being "cluttered with detail." I've certainly found myself there: researching something that's of tangential relevance to what I'm doing, so that at the end of the day I've worked hard all day long and accomplished... Well... Not much. But it's an easy trap to slip into, because it feels good to be busy.

I once had a conversation with a colleague about billing. He said that he'd spent an entire hour staring out of his office window and thinking about a case, and he came up with an approach and strategy that simplified a difficult issue, one that substantially increased the client's chances of success. His conundrum? How to bill for time spent staring and thinking—

as well as how to find more of that time and how to protect it since he didn't appear to be "busy" but he was in fact very productive.

> **We seem to live in a culture that embraces busyness and has made it a virtue to be busy. And yet, I'm taken by the idea that being busy can mean being "cluttered with detail."**

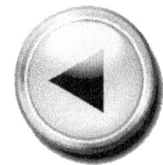

The law actually recognizes this distinction in billing rates. A 1st or 2nd year associate is billed at a lower rate than a more senior associate or partner because (among other reasons) experience teaches a lawyer how to use her time most productively; the work accomplished in an hour by a senior associate is almost certainly more useful (i.e. more productive) than that accomplished in the same hour by a new associate. And yet, both may appear to be equally busy.

When someone describes working a lot without getting the results he wants, I often suggest he ask, "Am I busy, or am I productive?" The question is an adjunct of the Quadrant time/priority management system that Stephen Covey teaches, and it takes that system to the next level because the question makes manifest the danger of working on an important task without being productive.

This question is particularly appropriate for practice/career management issues. For example, in the course of a job search, is it busy or productive to spend hours reading ads on a job board? The answer likely depends on the board and on whether there's follow–up to an ad of interest. It's also appropriate in substantive practice at times to question whether certain activities are productive or whether they're just generating work.

So, consider devoting a few minutes today to checking over your task list, or to reflecting on how you spent your time last week, and ask, "Am I busy, or am I productive?"

Seven Tips to Turn Your Commute into Valuable Time

Very few people have short commutes these days. I know of only one woman who lives within 15 minutes of her office, regardless of the time of day she makes the trip—and that's because she's only a 15-minute walk away. The rest of us put up with anywhere from 30 minutes to a couple of hours a day in commuting, time that often feels wasted. A few years ago, I lost my 20-minute one-way commute when I moved to a lovely house that was at least 45 minutes from the office. If I traveled during busy traffic times (not even rush hour, just busy) the drive time swelled to a minimum of an hour and twenty minutes and often longer. I was not happy. Nor was I alone; in 2005, the U.S. Census Bureau estimated that Americans spend more than 100 hours commuting to work each year—substantially more time than the 80 hours many of us are entitled to spend on vacation.

Most of us hop in the car, listen to the radio or a CD, grind our teeth (or worse) as we try to cope with traffic, and essentially move through the commute time mindlessly. But it doesn't have to be that way.

I've learned some ways to use that travel time to my benefit, either personally or professionally. These tips assume that you're driving; you have many more options if you're able to take mass transit or to carpool, which most lawyers can't, just because of the uncertainty of working hours.

1. **Podcasts**. There are tons of terrific podcasts that will enrich your life, both professionally and personally. On the professional side, check out David Maister's work, available at http://davidmaister.com/podcasts/.

These podcasts are organized by topic and each is an incisive, immensely practical, and even entertaining take on topics of importance to professionals. The Wall Street Journal offers a variety of podcasts that will get you up to speed on news, financial issues, and some lifestyle trends. And NPR always has something new and interesting.

To find podcasts that interest you, visit Podcast Alley or the iTunes Podcast page. You can find podcasts about current events, religion, history, entertainment, spirituality, and much more. Sample some and see what piques your interest. It's amazing what you can learn that will be helpful immediately in your professional life, what you can contribute to your next cocktail party conversation, and what might inspire you.

2. **Books on CD**. If you don't have time to catch up on the latest best-sellers, this might be the answer. Audio books are available at most libraries or you can buy them. My favorite solutions are Simply Audiobooks, which is a Netflix-style rental-by-mail service and its cousin, Audiobooks.com, with unlimited downloads.

3. **Thinking time: Plan (or review) your day, practice for an argument, mull over potential case strategies, etc.** It's often difficult to get time to stare out the window and just think, and yet that's one of the most valuable things we can do. If you spend commuting time contemplating a particular legal point—what are the downfalls of the argument you're considering, and what's the risk/benefit analysis?—you will often find that the time is profitable. Even if it's just mentally organizing yourself for your day or your evening, thinking time in the car will allow you to make better use of your time in the office or at home. Keep your cell phone handy (hands-free, please) so you can leave yourself a voicemail with your brilliant conclusions, or invest in a microcassette or digital recorder if you have an assistant who can transcribe your thoughts for future reference. Commuting time is also a good opportunity to reflect on your goals, and whether you're moving

closer to attaining them.

4. **Learn something.** If you're a lifelong learner, this tip might be for you. Invest in audios of lectures on history, philosophy, business, science, whatever tickles your fancy. The Teaching Company has some fascinating offerings.

5. **Relaxation time.** Traffic isn't relaxing. But if you surround yourself with music you enjoy, make sure you have hot coffee or cold water, optimize your car seat for comfort, and—most importantly—optimize your attitude, it can be somewhat relaxing. Decide not to worry about getting ahead through traffic since more often than not, arriving at your destination five minutes later than you'd hoped won't change the course of your day. (If it does, decrease your stress level and leave earlier.) Drive mindfully, noticing the sights you pass, the colors of the sky, what people in cars around you are doing.

6. **Vent.** Especially when you're driving home, take time during your commute to rehash the day's events and to vent any frustration you may be carrying. Don't bring the toxicity into your home; instead, take your private time in the car to say whatever you'd like to whomever you'd like without any negative consequences. Just don't be surprised when folks in other cars look your way and giggle. And don't get so wrapped up in your venting that you succumb to road rage.

7. **Think about whether you should move closer to work.** As you drive mindfully, notice the neighborhoods you pass. Perhaps one of them should be home for you. According to Robert Putnam, author of *Bowling Alone*, every 10 minutes you add to your commute causes a 10% decrease in the amount of time you devote to your family and your community. There's a psychic toll as well as a financial toll.

Each of these tips will help to minimize the commuting burden and to maximize the pleasure and efficiency you experience at work and at play. The key is in making conscious decisions on how to use your time.

Avoid Overwhelm: Hit Reset

A client recently called me, and I could hear the tension in his voice right away. Too many projects coming due at the same time (and thus, another long weekend in the office) combined with sheer exhaustion to make Rick an unhappy lawyer. "I just don't know how I'm going to get it all done. I always do, but you know, I'm thinking maybe I'm not going to pull it off this time." We started listing out exactly what Rick needed to do and, while it was a lot of work, the truth was that he could accomplish all of it within about 30 hours, which would leave him some time free over the weekend—if, and only if, he was able to stop worrying about the work and start doing it.

"So, Rick," I ventured, "you sound completely stressed out, and your brain seems to be going in six different ways at once. Why don't you hit the reset button?"

Rick took a few seconds before speaking, and when he did his voice was incredulous, laced with frustration–bordering–on–anger. "And how would you recommend I do THAT?"

We all fall into periods of overwhelm, frustration, malaise, boredom, and so on. Sometimes it's a few minutes, and other times the feelings can last for weeks. Hitting the reset button is a simple technique I recommend. Every person I've ever talked with has something that serves as the human equivalent of Ctrl–Alt–Delete. (Sorry, Mac users, you'll have to translate that into Mac language or remember your PC days!) And most people have a variety of strategies that may work, depending on the situation. A few that clients and I have used:

- Going for a walk, a run, a bike ride, or other solitary exercise
- Playing music that pumps you up (or soothes you)
- Yoga
- Calling a friend or loved one for a short conversation
- Flipping through vacation photos
- Meditating, praying, or deep breathing
- Getting a cup of coffee, tea, or other beverage of your choice and savoring it
- Using scents (essential oils, for instance) to trigger relaxation
- Stretching
- Making a "gratitude list"

Although each of the activities listed above are fairly quick and designed for run–of–the–mill circumstances, hitting reset can also mean taking a weekend trip, taking a weekly class, or something else that's sufficiently out of the ordinary to break your routine. Each year, I spend a week alone in Wyoming, walking and thinking in nature. When I return from my retreat, I see my business and my life through new eyes.

After Rick and I explored some ideas, he decided that he would take a quick walk around the block while listening to a favorite "power song" as soon as we hung up, and that he would make time to play ball with his son for a few minutes in the evening. He was skeptical but willing to give "the reset" a shot. And he discovered that it worked well enough that he now "hits reset" regularly, as soon as he starts feeling overwhelmed or otherwise on edge.

What might you do when you need to reset your system?

Top 10 Tips to Overcome Overwhelm

Overwhelm can tank a day faster than just about anything else When you have more email than you can handle, an out–of–control task list, and phone calls that just won't stop, it's almost impossible to operate effectively. Even if you manage to limp along, you may find that you're distracted and that things are falling through the cracks. Over the years, I've honed in on a variety of methods to beat overwhelm, and these are the top 10, based on my own experience and client feedback:

Move. Overwhelm tends to cause paralysis, and the fastest fix is a quick burst of activity. Walk around the block or your office floor, dance for 30 seconds (close the door!), or do 10 jumping jacks. Get your blood pumping.

Lift your mood. Overwhelm brings a heavy energy. Use music, fresh flowers, aromas, or whatever works for you to get a lift I keep a bottle of orange essential oil at my desk because I find that a drop or two perks me up almost instantly.

Focus intently for a short time. After my computer and telephone, my most–used piece of equipment is a digital timer. When I feel stuck, I'll set the timer for 45 minutes and power through that time, knowing that I can take a break as soon as the timer beeps. I also compete against myself using the timer to see how quickly I can sort through papers or complete other dreaded tasks. The timer gets me going, and I usually keep going (thanks to momentum) even after the alarm sounds.

Clean it up. Clutter reduces productivity and creates overwhelm. If your desk is messy, set aside 15 minutes to clear it off, even if that means stacking papers and moving them to the floor If your email in-box is so full that you feel anxious when you open it, set aside an hour to tame it.

Call in the reinforcements. Find the right help for your source of overwhelm. Perhaps your assistant can help you clear your desk, or a colleague may be able to give you feedback to help cut through the mental clutter. When you feel overwhelmed, it's hard to see outside the bubble of stress Get some help.

Dump it. One common source of overwhelm is the mental task list. When you're juggling "must do" items in your head, fighting to remember all of them, you're pulling energy away from productive activity to simple memory maintenance Do a brain dump and get the tasks on paper and free up your mind for more useful work.

Get out of the office and do something else. Admittedly, you can't always implement this tip, but it can be very effective. Have you ever noticed how often brilliant ideas strike while you're in the shower, running, walking the dog, or doing other activities unrelated to work? When the body is working and the mind is free to wander, creativity flourishes.

Access a different part of your brain. One litigator I know uses art to focus himself before a trial. Art allows him to pull back from the logical, analytical side of his brain and bring forward the emotional and creative parts. What can you do to bring another part of your skills to the table?

Mind map. If you're searching for an elusive link between facts or trying to form a creative argument, try using a mind map. Get a clean piece of paper, draw a circle in the middle of the page and label it with the problem or circumstance you're contemplating. Think about related subjects, actions you could take, and people who might be helpful in addressing the issue, and draw lines and branches to represent the ideas that come up. If you're really stuck you may find a mind map more useful than an ordinary list.

If you've tried several of these approaches unsuccessfully, you may be

exhausted. Think of your energy as a pitcher of water. If you pour and pour and pour without replenishment, the pitcher will empty and nothing you try (except adding more water) will allow it to pour more. If a quick break or quick spurt of energy doesn't refresh you, your pitcher may be dangerously close to empty. Identifying that spot and taking action is a critical professional competency.

Seven Foundations of Time Mastery for Attorneys

Time–Saving Resources

The Internet is replete with time–saving resources. The following are some of my favorites:

1. **Mozy.com online computer back–up system**: A few years ago, I suffered through three hard drive crashes in about 6 months. I try to back up my files to an external hard drive regularly, but sometimes I slip up and forget. Mozy.com is an inexpensive Internet–based backup system that operates automatically. When my Outlook file got corrupted a few months ago and I somehow had neglected to back up those files to the external drive, Mozy rescued me from disaster. I think of it as cheap insurance and a time saver in case disaster strikes. Be sure to consider implications before backing up privileged information. (Mozy.com)

2. **Ta–da Lists**: Getting to "to do" list out of my head is critical. It's easy to forget something important otherwise, and it's a waste to devote valuable attention to trying to remember "must do" items. Ta–da Lists is an easy, web–based solution that will allow you to access your lists anywhere, and you can share your list with others (perhaps with an assistant) if you so choose. (TaDaList.com)

3. **YouSendIt.com**: When you need to send large files, YouSendIt is an easy solution. You can choose from several service levels, including a free option that offers only basic function and more advanced levels that offer password protection, tracking, and more. Again, be sure to

Seven Foundations of Time Mastery for Attorneys

consider whether to send privileged information in this way. (YouSendIt.com)

4. **Online relaxation and meditation timer**: Practice can be stressful, and sometimes a short break can make all the difference—not just in your stress level, but also in your productivity. "My Free Guided Meditation" allows you to set a timer for 1 to 60 minutes, accompanied (if you like) with a selection of relaxing music. It's an easy way to design a quick, time-limited break. (myfreeguidedmeditation.com/)

5. **Healthy meals, cooked for you.** Too busy to cook, and sick of the same-old, same-old options? Look into prepared foods for pick-up or delivery. Try a Google search on "healthy meal delivery service" and your city to see what's available. Though these options aren't inexpensive, it's a much better alternative to night after night of greasy take-out.

6. **Read It Later:** When you surf across an interesting link but don't have time to read it, you might bookmark it. If you do so, though, you'll quickly find that your bookmarks grow unwieldy, and clearing them out may be so time-consuming that you won't want to bother. Enter Read It Later, which allows you to mark a page for later reading, even offline. All it takes is a click (once you've installed the application into your browser), and you're good to go. You can even read your saved pages offline, and there are apps for the iPhone, iPad, Droid, Blackberry®—you get the idea. (ReadItLater.com)

Julie A. Fleming, J.D., A.C.C. is the founder of Life at the Bar LLC. Julie practiced law (specializing in patent litigation) for over fifteen years, in firms ranging from two to more than 2100 lawyers, before founding Life at the Bar LLC in 2005. She provides attorney development coaching, focusing on topics such as leadership development, rainmaking, professional development, career strategy, and work/life integration, and is a frequent speaker for law firms, law schools, and bar associations. Julie also publishes the weekly email newsletter, *Leadership Matters for Lawyers*. Additional information and resources are available at www.lifeatthebar.com. Julie may be contacted by email to jaf@lifeatthebar.com or by telephone to 800.758.6214, ext. 1.

www.ingramcontent.com/pod-product-compliance
Lightning Source LLC
Chambersburg PA
CBHW081217230426
43666CB00015B/2775